*The Last
House
of Ulster*

The Last House of Ulster

A Family in Belfast

CHARLES FORAN

A Saturday Night Book
HarperCollins*Publishers*Ltd

Lyrics from "Four Green Fields" by Tommy Makem, Tin Whistle
Music, B.M.I. Reprinted with kind permission.

Portion from "In Belfast" reprinted from *Night-Crossing* by Derek
Mahon, © Oxford University Press 1968, reprinted by permission of
Oxford University Press.

Portion from "Funeral Rites" reprinted from *North* by Seamus
Heaney, by permission of Faber and Faber Ltd.

First edition

Canadian Cataloguing in Publication Data

Foran, Charles, 1960-
The last house of Ulster : a family in Belfast

"A Saturday night book."
ISBN 0-00-255311-2

1. McNally family.   2. Belfast (Northern Ireland) – Social life and
customs.   3. Violence – Northern Ireland – Belfast.   4. Northern
Ireland – Politics and government – 1969-   I. Title.

DA995.B5F6 1995   941.6'70824'0922   C94-932390-X

95 96 97 98 99 ❖ RRD 10 9 8 7 6 5 4 3 2

Printed and bound in the United States

for Anna and Claire

One part of my mind must learn to know its place —
The things that happen in the kitchen-houses
And echoing back-streets of this desperate city
Should engage more than my casual interest,
Exact more interest than my casual pity.

from "In Belfast"
Derek Mahon

INTRODUCTION

In August 1992, my wife, Mary, and I were in Dublin for a vacation when we decided to rent a car and drive up to Belfast. The plan was to visit a family I had known for fourteen years. While the idea was unexceptional — I had been to the city many times before — two factors would make this journey unique. First, a car had become necessary after a bomb in a train station closed the Dublin–Belfast line. My previous forays into the North had involved trains and buses, or else riding as a car passenger. Never had I driven myself. Second, we would be bringing our eighteen-month-old daughter with us. Friends in Dublin had offered to mind Anna for the day, but I wouldn't hear of it. Like any father, I wanted to show off my child. Like any parent, however, I also didn't want her shot by a sniper or wounded in an explosion.

The logic, or illogic, of my reasoning sat me down in astonishment. I had requested a children's car seat. When none proved available, I was outraged; no responsible North American parent would think of driving even to a corner store with an unsecured child. I demanded that the rental company go out and buy us a seat. They did, and I proceeded to drive my daughter into a military police state patrolled by 28,000 heavily armed security forces. . . . More rationally, my hesitation smacked of a betrayal of the Belfast family. I had been visiting them since I was nineteen. I had gone up to their house on the heels of political assassinations, in the midst of prisoner campaigns and marching seasons, in the wake of bombings and slayings. Now I was going up for lunch, with Mary, a veteran (she and I met while studying in Dublin), and Anna, a debutante.

I drove my family due north along the eastern seaboard of Ireland, across the border, towards Belfast. Within an hour of departing the Irish capital I had internalized my doubts, suppressed my hesitations and was enjoying a curious light-headedness. I had, I decided, no choice but to make the trip; the responsibility for it fell squarely on my shoulders. I was being wilful. I was surrendering to fate. I was getting on with my life. Life, if it wanted, might get all over me. For my Northern Irish friends, the dizziness that resulted from pondering these incongruities formed a state of mind; the trials and tribulations that must have resulted from coexisting with such incongruities surely constituted a way of life. Finally, at age thirty-two, I realized where they had been all their lives.

For this family had raised five children in North Belfast. The oldest child was an adolescent when the Troubles started, the youngest a six-year-old boy. The parents, both Belfast-reared, had known one city; after August 1969, they had to learn about a new one. I will call the family the McNallys, and will change names and alter details to guard their privacy. Not that their experiences of the last quarter-century are especially noteworthy. By their own admission, open to compassionate dispute, they have gotten off lightly; by the standards of their community, open to examination by specialists in post-traumatic stress syndrome, the family has managed fine. From my newly found perspective, what these people had lived through was extraordinary; the qualities of character the parents possessed in themselves and nurtured in their children were noteworthy; the terrible decision taken by a mother about the future of her sons and daughters within the North needed to be told and understood in context.

The Last House of Ulster may appear to be a blur of journeys, a litany of comings and goings. Ultimately, though, the narrative aspires to go nowhere: to circle around a certain corner of Belfast, a certain neighbourhood and street, a certain house. Most of our lives are spent in a few rooms, after all — a kitchen and bedroom, the chamber known as the family room or sitting room or, in Canadian suburbs, the den. Even my one proper travel experience, a car ride from Dublin, will end up exploring a reconstructed map of a Toronto neighbourhood circa the 1960s and 70s, as much as the highways of counties Louth and Down circa 1992. Anyone familiar with the distilled qualities of the Irish landscape, especially its staggering history-per-square-metre ratio, will sympathize with this tendency to glance back or even look inward while still keeping an eye on the road.

The title of this book riffs on a piece of Irish music. Traditional music is generally cyclical. However many parts a piece may contain, in order for it to work it is obliged to repeat itself, to begin again. In music, the repetitions are called "rounds", and if the night is good, the more the merrier. In Belfast, even taking into account the optimism emerging from the recent ceasefire, the cycle of political intransigence and violent sectarianism is called the status quo — hardly worth celebrating in a title.

But I'm actually thinking of something else. On display in the Northern Ireland house I know best are qualities that, grounded in routine and celebrated through repetition, are instinctively joyful. As I grow older, the persistence of these qualities gives me great, possibly inordinate cheer.

PART I

CHAPTER I

I phoned the McNallys from Dublin. Even the syncopated ring — rr-rr, rr-rr — stirred memories. Maureen picked up on the third beat.

She called me by my old name.

"Are you home today?" I asked.

Maureen McNally oched. It was like a sigh or a tch, only more bemused, weary. Her och meant: Of course, Never any doubt, Sure where else would we be? She offered the standard family joke: "Why would anyone want to visit this awful place?"

"Not the place," I dutifully answered. "You and James. The house, too."

"God love you."

"Besides, I want you to meet Anna."

"We'll have a bite of lunch ready," she promised.

"Don't go to any trouble."

"You're most welcome."

Maureen passed the receiver to her husband. James enquired about Mary and Anna, my parents, myself. His voice was bright and cheery; his laugh was booming; he seemed in the best of form. He always sounded that way, though.

"Do you remember how to get to the house?"

I said I did.

"We'll sit down for a meal," he said.

"Don't go to —"

"No trouble at all."

"A few rashers?" I asked.

"And a drop of tea."

"Big job."

"Indeed."

We laughed.

"But you're not obliged," he added. "Just talking on the phone is grand."

"Would you mind?"

"You're all most welcome."

I knew that. Few open offers of hospitality felt as sincere. Certainly no others meant as much to me.

Did I remember how to get to the McNally house? I remembered the promontory of a mountain that backdropped a lower North Belfast suburb. I remembered a neighbourhood along the western slope of the mountain, and a tree-lined street in the heart of the neighbourhood, and a red-brick house near the middle blocks of the street. I remembered the low fence and gated driveway outside the house; the curtained bay windows and red panelled door facing the road. I remembered every room behind the windows and door, every stick of furniture in each of the rooms. The ring of the telephone. The aroma of the fire. The taste of grilled potato bread.

I first saw Belfast from the window of a train, the glass streaked by rain, in early September 1979. Four of us disembarked at York Road station. Two girls, one a McNally and the other a friend, and two guys, one a McNally cousin from Canada and the other a friend. Belfast had met up with Toronto at a music festival in Donegal. "You'll know us by our red wellies," Bernie McNally had assured her cousin Pat on the phone. Both girls had dutifully sloshed through the Buncrana muck in neon-red boots. Pat, however, hadn't understood his relative's accent, leaving us without a visual aid. This particular McNally had, he recalled from a photo, long black hair and blue eyes. Her cheeks were ruddy. Her skin was alabaster.

We studied faces. Irish women, we soon realized, tended to have long black hair and blue eyes, or else long orange hair and brown eyes. They tended to have alabaster skin but high colour, especially in the cheeks. They often had freckles. In 1979, moreover, Irish women wore red wellington boots to traditional music festivals in Donegal.

Happily, Pat and I were easier to pick out of a crowd — with our three-storey rucksacks and silly tweed caps. Bernie McNally flagged us down in a mud bath masquerading as a camping ground. She looked like her photo. Her friend Una, in contrast, had carrot hair and almond eyes. Una seemed to blush constantly. Her face and arms were smeared in freckles.

They began speaking. It sounded like this: *Arr ggg nay wee dnn? Aye, ddd nay weee, rrr!*

"Hi," we both said.

Privately, Pat and I compared tallies. I had located one English word: "wee". He had taken respite in "aye". Bernie had asked, twice, if we were ready to go.

"Aye," said Pat.

"Wee," I added.

We boarded a bus for Derry. Conversation was full of random wees and cryptic ayes. It was also punctuated by puzzled pauses and furtive consultations between partners. The Belfast side had an advantage: we sounded like American television. And Pat, raised by Northern Irish parents, had a softer ear. My position was straightforward: for the most part, I hadn't a clue what these girls were saying.

Besides, we were about to cross the border from the Republic of Ireland into Northern Ireland, and I wanted a moment to steel myself. What a month we'd chosen to tour the island. Earlier that week, the IRA had ambushed a British army patrol outside Warrenpoint, County Down. Eighteen soldiers were killed, the largest single death toll since 1969. An English tourist caught in the crossfire had upped the tally.

County Down was in the North, of course, where there was a conflict, where these things happened. But that same day, as Pat and I were hitchhiking through Connemara, a radio-triggered IRA bomb blew up a boat at Mullaghmore, near Sligo town. Casualties included Lord Mountbatten and his grandson, the Dowager Lady Brabourne and a fourteen-year-old boy. We had passed through the area the following morning, looking for the grave of W.B. Yeats. Traffic was slowed by checkpoints; villages were crawling with army. Yet County Sligo was not in the North. It wasn't even part of historic Ulster. The county was one of twenty-six in the Republic, where there wasn't a conflict, where these things usually didn't happen.

That assurance had struck my nineteen-year-old mind as remarkable. The island wasn't that much larger than Nova Scotia. How could one distinguish utterly the world of Antigonish from that of Kentville? How could one speak with confidence that troubles in Dartmouth wouldn't spill over into Halifax? They must have an impervious border in Ireland, I decided: brick walls and barbed wire, elaborate screening techniques. Irish people must have a different sense of space.

Next thing I knew, the bus had pulled into Derry, or Londonderry, or whatever the city was called, and I had somehow missed the impervious border. (A soldier had waved the bus through a checkpoint.) Bernie assured me the train ride to Belfast would be more interesting. "A good long ride it is," she said.

I checked my map.

"About seventy miles," I said.

"That long?"

"This is my first time in Derry," offered Una. "It's meant to be a grand big city."

I checked my guidebook.

"About 80,000 people," I said.

"That many?"

On the train, kids next to us in the no-smoking end of the car smoked cigarettes and played their portable radio so loudly they couldn't hear the conductor's request to turn it down. Beyond the rain-fogged glass was the same Irish idyll we had passed through in the

Republic. The earth was green, the buildings — farmhouses and churches, villages — were grey. The countryside rolled down into valleys and climbed up hills; fields were flecked by sheep and cows, dotted with ruins. Farmers wandered paths alone or with a dog. Tractors puffed along lanes. To the passing glance, the landscape appeared lush and sleepy. A Union Jack above a doorway in a railway station caught my eye. It seemed anomalous, out of place.

Then a city emerged. Not hurriedly: a few outlying housing estates, blocks of shops, wider and busier roads. As they often did in Ireland, fields and farms penetrated the urban landscape almost until the centre of town. When the countryside vanished in this case, however, it did so with a vengeance; the train was soon surrounded by brick and asphalt. Judging from the explosions of graffiti, the passing glimpses of army patrols and police checkpoints, it was a distinctive city, too.

The conductor entered the car. First, he meekly mentioned the no-smoking policy to the kids. Then he proudly announced York station. Belfast city centre. End of the line.

"You must be knackered," Bernie said to me.

"Knackered?"

"From the long trip," she explained.

"From Canada?"

"Derry."

The train ride had taken two hours. "I'll be all right," I assured her.

Mairtin McNally, the eldest son, was supposed to collect us at the station. We waited ten minutes. Bernie rang home. "There's been a delay," she explained.

"The car?" asked Una.

"Aye."

"Did they push it?"

"Father, Mairtin and Sean were last seen chasing the Granada down the road," she admitted.

Finally, a battered blue Granada pulled up to the curb. The driver gunned the engine. Then he unrolled the passenger-side window.

"Sorry, Bernie," he said.

"You got her going?"

"Took a while."

"Will we make it?"

"I don't think we'll leave her to idle long."

The four of us piled in. Mairtin, the driver, revved the engine again before pressing down on the clutch. Bernie introduced the visitors.

"What about you?" asked Mairtin.

"Hi," we both said.

"How was the trip?"

I hesitated.

"Long," answered Bernie.

"We're knackered," said Una.

"Cup of tea will do you right," decided Mairtin.

Television images of Belfast living painted an unlovely picture. Typically, the shot was of a narrow street of identical terraced dwellings, chimneys in military formation, doors opening onto sidewalks. Concrete textures went unrelieved by grass, let alone trees. The sky was socked-in grey, the light was smoky grey. Even the drizzle — it was always raining in Belfast — had a hue: off-grey. On camera, these houses looked downtrodden and poor. Humans inhabiting them naturally assumed similar characteristics. Beleaguered housewives stood in doorframes burping babies and scolding toddlers. Unshaven husbands with liquid eyes hovered in the hallway. Old fellas blushed alcohol in the kitchen. Journalist-prompted complaints were desperate, humour was dire and views were no compromise, no surrender. With accents largely incomprehensible, however, the North American viewer was left with the image of a scrappy people huddled in their mean little houses.

"You're very welcome," said Maureen, as we climbed out of the car after a short ride.

"Thanks," I said.

"You're welcome here," added James.

"Thanks."

A young man shook my hand. He said his name was Sean. He said we were very welcome in the house.

I thanked him too.

"Who's for tea?" asked Maureen.

"Let's get them inside first, dear," suggested James.

"Thanks," said Pat.

"You're welcome."

We were ushered into the house.

"You must be starved after the long journey," said Maureen.

"It really wasn't all that —"

"A drop of tea will do you right," said James.

"I'll put the kettle on," said his wife.

Formal introductions followed. Besides the parents, we met five children: Mairtin and Sean, Patricia and Bernie, and the youngest boy, Ciaran. Though they all still lived at home, and all except Patricia were still in school, the McNally "kids" ranged in age from seventeen to twenty-six. The kids were adults. The parents were older adults. It was a family of grown-ups.

It was also a family of hosts. Within an hour, my head was reeling. Offers poured in: to carry my rucksack upstairs, to show me the toilet, to fetch some towels, to explain the immersion heater. I could do a load of wash if I wanted. I could have a bath, a shower, a lie-down. A cup of tea was waiting. A cup of tea was poured. And there were scones and biscuits. To tide me over until the meal was ready. Until the table was set.

Good hosts asked questions. How was the trip (from Canada, not Derry)? How was the festival? Was I enjoying Ireland? Did I mind the rain? And my parents — were they well? I had one brother, one sister, did I? And they were well too? Also in school? Working in a bank? That must be very interesting. Toronto must be an interesting city. Canada must be an interesting place. Cold, reported Maureen's sister. Wicked in the winter.

"Short growing season, I understand," she said.

"Growing season?"

"For flowers."

I heard this: *flahhrrs*.

"*Flahhrrs*?" I repeated.

"I couldn't stick it," declared Maureen.

But the attention wasn't lavished exclusively on guests. The McNallys treated each other in a particular manner. Everyone poured everyone else tea. Everyone offered everyone else a biscuit. At dinner, the children waited on the parents. Daughters insisted their mother sit while the food was brought in. Sons refilled their father's glass. In conversation, parents solicited the opinions of children and then waited for them to answer. Younger family members fell silent while an older sibling spoke; all nodded respectfully at the thoughts of their father or mother. People said Please and Thank You and Are You All Right Yourself? Before bed, everyone offered to fix everyone else a water bottle, a cup of tea, a few rounds of toast. No one was encouraged to be first up to put on the kettle; everyone offered to do it.

What kind of a family was this?

My travelling companion filled in the blanks that night. The McNallys were a middle-class Catholic family. The father owned a pub in a town outside Belfast. The mother worked part-time in a local shop. Patricia, the eldest daughter, was a nurse in a city hospital. Mairtin was an engineering student. Sean studied commerce. Bernie had just written her A-levels, and was hoping to join her brothers at the Ulster Polytechnic, and Ciaran was still in high school. The house we were in, a three-storey rowhouse with narrow hallways and small rooms, a tiny front yard and a back garden rendered impenetrable by lines of hanging wash, was temporary. The McNallys had lived in better houses before. They would be moving again, soon.

Mairtin McNally invited Pat and me to a pub the next afternoon. Born in 1954, Mairtin was a compact man with a boyish face, a quick smile and marine-blue eyes that protruded from their sockets. A mop of black hair, seventies-style long and banged, lent the face a roundness at odds with his wishbone cheeks. Mairtin's smile fanned ripples across his cheeks and splayed the corners of his eyes. All the McNally men were slim and compact. All had athletic physiques; all played sports; all excelled. Among them, Mairtin had perhaps the slightest build. His stomach was concave and his shoulders were narrow. His hands were tiny. But his arms were sinewy with veins; his grip was punishing. He dangled his arms at his sides when he walked, as if they were numb. When he sat, he kept perfectly still: no jiggly leg, no gestures. Even relaxed — slouching in a chair, arms cupped behind his head — he seemed alert and watchful.

To get to the pub, we needed the car. To get the car to run, Pat and I soon discovered, we had to do some running ourselves. Mairtin tried the engine first; it coughed, went grrr, then died. Ordering Patricia behind the wheel, he joined us at the back fender. The problem, he explained, was temperament. The Granada, with rust roseolas along the doorframes and a rotten fuel-injection system, disliked damp weather. It preferred a drier climate — sunny Andalusia, temperate Provence. But the rain hadn't let up all last night. Actually, it had been raining off and on for almost a week.

"Wrong car for Belfast," summarized Patricia.

"Put her into neutral, Tricia."

"Right."

Mairtin hitched up his pants. "Push, lads," he advised.

Though it sloped gently down, the road was bookended by larger streets that seemed to climb a gradient. We pushed the Granada towards a traffic light visible through wisps of fog a hundred metres ahead. Patricia revved the engine. Twice it turned over; twice it sputtered when she tried shifting into gear. Towards the corner, I was running flat out and the trunk metal was barely beneath my fingers.

The light was green.

"Fuck it," said Mairtin, suddenly straightening.

"It'll catch," I wheezed.

"Stop the car, Patricia!"

"Don't!"

"Stop the —"

The car stopped. On the first white line. On a still-green light.

"We'll have to back her up," said Mairtin.

"Why?"

"It's easiest."

The light changed to yellow.

Patricia got out of the car. "We're not welcome there," she said, indicating across the road.

"Not our neighbourhood," added Mairtin.

Across the road was a housing estate of white stucco exteriors and red tile roofs. The houses looked tidy but slightly worn. On the gable wall facing the intersection was a mural of King Billy* on his rearing horse, with the words "REMEMBER 1690" below him. Curbstones on either sidewalk were painted red, white and blue.

The light turned red.

We shifted around to the front hood. Both my pant legs were patterned with sprays of water, courtesy of the sluicing tires. Slowly we pushed the Granada back up the incline to the house. Then we tried again. This time, it caught well before the light. Patricia pulled the parking brake. She got out, we got in.

"Where's the pub?" I asked, thirsty.

"No pub," answered Pat.

"I thought you might like to know what the crack really is," said Mairtin.

"The crack?"

Pat had kept the true itinerary secret. Never mind a drink, he now implied: we were off on a tour of Belfast, and our guide knew the city as none of his siblings or his parents knew it. Because, he had explained the night before, Mairtin had a history. He'd become involved. He'd even gone inside. Because, as I soon found out, the eldest McNally child had a gaze that burned through me and a totalizing view of the world that made my scalp sweat.

He also had a hushed speaking voice and a mouth-of-marbles accent. In a moving car, with the windows down, his every word was a strain to hear. My friend took the front seat. I was stuck in the back.

"No use staying in the house," Mairtin whispered. "Have to get out, you know. The Brits are occupying the country. They're waging war. On us. On our people. It's fucking dire, to tell the truth. Fucking dire."

"Yes," Pat and I answered.

War zones materialized beyond the windshield. We passed streets of bricked-up houses and burnt-out pubs, shops and offices protected by wire-meshed windows and caged doorways. Whole city blocks lay

---

A glossary of phrases and names begins on page 205.

derelict. Empty lots hosted piles of furniture — couches and chairs, baby cribs — neatly arranged, as if the homes around them had vaporized. Automobile carcasses, many not so recently torched, hunkered by curbs. We passed bunker high schools and fortress social-services offices. Police stations were imprisoned behind brick walls and scrolls of concertina wire; a courthouse was heavily defended; a Dickensian prison looked more concerned with invaders than escapees. Housing estates boasted impromptu barricades, now piles of garbage. Litter swirled over sidewalks. Glintings of bottle glass speckled the pavement.

On every brick fence, seemingly, every exposed surface, was graffiti; on the sides of many buildings — called gable walls — were murals.

Mairtin's occupiers also obliged. Army vehicles rumbled up and down the main roads, twin sentries poking up from hatches, their automatic rifles pointed at random targets. At a stoplight, the Granada was swarmed by a foot patrol pouring out of a nearby station. With their full combat gear, visored helmets and gleaming black weapons, these men didn't look like police officers walking the beat. They weren't; they were an army in the heart of enemy country. Mairtin lowered his gaze when the patrol passed. He also made a U-turn to avoid a roadblock. It was RUC-operated, but from a distance these men and this operation didn't look much like a local police action either — flak jackets and automatic rifles, armoured Land Rovers and crouching snipers.

And his people? The city teemed as only cities with narrow streets, high population densities and centralized shopping areas can. Sidewalks were packed. Men clustered at corners, cigarettes dangling from their mouths, hands pocketed. Women grappled with shopping bags and children. Car traffic flowed but pram lanes were jammed. Mothers wore track suits and weary smiles. Toddlers sat upright in the seats, the better to eat their sweets; babies slept through the din. Despite the congestion, shops further reduced sidewalk space by displaying their wares out front — blackened potatoes and dirt-crusted carrots, sacks of coal. Butchers, goods bleeding in the window, boasted queues to the door. One posted a sign beneath a tray of chopped steak: NO TEETH REQUIRED.

It was Saturday, and Belfast — or what I thought was Belfast — looked full of people, all reasonably busy, reasonably calm.

That didn't seem right. Besides the presence of the occupiers, Mairtin's route kept crisscrossing fearsome sectarian divides. Only his attitude behind the wheel in certain neighbourhoods — cautious, shifting gears with quiet fury — and his even more hushed voice hinted at any unease. To the uninformed eye, street scenes in Catholic ghettos blended with those in Protestant ghettos. The peace lines he so purposefully showed us segregated identical terraced estates, cloned dwellings, uniform shops. To the uninformed eye, the city we drove through was a study in sameness: same shabby neighbourhoods, same low-end shops and businesses, same urban blight. Same black taxis and pasty white people. Same poverty and constriction.

Fucking dire? I thought so.

Nevertheless, Mairtin's narration rendered the various areas not only distinct but at odds. Streets a block apart were, in fact, religions, ideologies, histories apart. Shopping areas offering similar stock provided completely different services; one kind of resident bought there, another didn't. The drab hues of Glencairn in no way resembled the drab hues of Ardoyne; if I looked closer, one neighbourhood was coloured Orange, the other Green. Nor were the army patrols in the Shankill the same as those along the Falls Road. Quite the opposite: in the Shankill, the army was the protector, the colluder; in the Falls, it was the attacker, the adversary.

I got no strong sense of war or peace, Orange or Green, our people or their people, from the backseat of the McNally car. First, there was the problem of perspective. Mine was definitely blinkered, and not just by the Granada roof. The sky sagged onto the tops of buildings. It was ashen, devoid of light, bloated with rain. It cloaked whatever lay farther along the slopes Mairtin kept ascending, then descending; it felt more like a ceiling. The higher up we drove, the denser grew the fog. From street level, the city was claustrophobic and thick, all red brick and grey stone, white stucco and corrugated tin. All built up. All broken down. All man-made and man-destroyed, too; nature was nowhere to be found.

Besides, overwhelming any oppositions was the single-minded ferocity of our guide. In orotund tones, half his words lost to hard Belfast consonants, Mairtin outlined a city in flames: kindled by injustice, fuelled by the hatred and mongering of the majority tribe, set alight by a foreign army. He spoke of neighbours burned out of their homes, businesses destroyed, jobs refused to qualified workers. Beatings and imprisonment, bombings and murders, were fires lit by systemic prejudices and historic wrongs. Violence, Mairtin was quick to add, meted out not to strangers, names in newspapers, but to people he knew — colleagues and friends, family.

His rage consumed itself at the gate to a cemetery near the top of the Falls Road. Milltown was resting place for thousands of ordinary Catholics. The graveyard was also where victims of the Troubles and selected participants in the Troubles were interred, often at the head of cortèges of balaclavaed, black-gloved paramilitaries firing commemorative rifle volleys into the air. Mairtin wanted us to see Milltown: where it was located, what it represented. The fog kept our eyes down. Stepping from the Granada, he indicated the arrowhead-shaped RUC station across the road, a stronghold decked out in tinted-window towers and surveillance cameras, and then he turned to the massive cemetery, its row upon row of headstones, memories overgrown in grass but still attended by the shrines of poor folk — plastic-covered portraits of saints, jam jars overflowing with dead daffodils; and Mairtin, ignoring the four-vehicle patrol pulling out of the station, fixed his gaze upon Pat and me and outstretched his arms, as if to embrace the oppression. "What are we supposed to do?" he asked passionately. "Answer me that — what are we supposed to do?"

Anger choked my replies, indignation sputtered any attempts at speech. Had there been an IRA application form in the car, I might have signed it.

On the way back to the house, I asked Mairtin to stop at a shop. Once inside the McNallys', Pat and I dutifully lied about the pub — "Great," we both intoned. Mairtin, I noticed, wasn't posed any questions.

I offered Maureen a gift.

"What are these?" she asked.

"*Flahhrrs*," I answered.

"Lovely," she said, smelling the bouquet.

"You're very welcome here," said her husband.

During our car tour, Mairtin McNally had pointed out two significant family landmarks. Near where we crossed the Crumlin Road was the neighbourhood where his father had grown up, above the family business. Mairtin's grandparents had emigrated to Belfast from a village south of Lough Neagh after Partition, country people hoping to better themselves. Few opportunities were available to their kind: no professions, no civil service, little or no work in the massive shipyards. (Harland and Wolff, who launched the *Titanic* in 1912, employed twenty thousand men.) Linen mills, however, the other pillar of Belfast industry, hired across the divide. Mill owners, in fact, went so far as to locate their businesses in the heart of working-class areas, both Catholic and Protestant. Most appealing about these settings was their proximity to neighbourhoods teeming with cheap, hungry labour. Twelve-hour shifts could commence at dawn. Saturdays could be treated like any other day.

Catholic spinners, largely women, drew bobbins of rove through troughs of boiling water. They worked barefoot in damp, unlit halls that were dim at the start of shifts, dark by the close of them. Protestant weavers, again mostly women, used their scissors to manipulate looms in thrashing noise and debilitating humidity. Weavers invented a sign language to communicate. By age thirty, they also developed foot-rot and arthritis, myopia and bad hearing. Boys signed on at the age of twelve as doffers, changing bobbins and helping set up machines. Adult men often stayed at home. One-quarter of working class Belfast was unemployed, and social security didn't exist. The mills paid poorly, but were still better than farming or domestic help.

John McNally opened a pub instead. He chose his location well: along the Crumlin Road, within a block of four mills and more than a thousand millworkers. Prospect Mill was majority Catholic. Rosebank Mill was evenly divided. The largest operation, Ewart's, tended to favour Protestants, as did the Edenderry across the road. (All the owners were Church of Ireland.) Typically, the make-up was happenstance:

grandfathers, fathers and sons worked side by side; friends got other friends hired on. Surrounding these tall buildings were blocks of shops and pubs. Some pubs drew from only one community: men from Ewart's might drink in Kilpatrick's, men from Prospect in the Rosebank bar. Others, like the Mountainview, had a mixed clientele. Almost all of the businesses were run by Catholics.

According to the Protestant moral lexicon, the entertainment industries — pubs and bookies, cinemas and dance halls — were disreputable. God-fearing people earned their living more uprightly. If such businesses had to exist, let the Catholics own them.

From 1928 onwards, the McNallys owned the Mountainview on Crumlin Road. John McNally died prematurely, leaving his wife and five children — including three-year-old James — on their own. A manager was hired. The family moved over the pub. Young James was now both fatherless and without a nation. Two of his older siblings had been born in the recalcitrant British colony of Ireland; his 1925 birthdate marked him as a citizen of a new entity. Some still called this place Ulster. Some called it the North or the Six Counties. Officially, the entity was known as Northern Ireland. Whatever its name, it was a statelet — with a parliament and a prime minister — that was also a part of the United Kingdom, with English currency as tender, the king and the Union Jack as symbols, and staggering local casualties in the First World War as recent proof of allegiance. Like his brothers and sisters, however, the boy understood himself still to be Irish, still to be a resident of Ireland. He understood himself rightly to belong in the place he was born, to be comfortable with the religion he practised, the history he learned.

In a strange way, the pub downstairs confirmed that sense of security. The Mountainview was the local for people from both communities. Mixing wasn't widespread — the position of the counter along one wall allowed customers to divide the floorspace — but the mood was friendly, even fraternal. Most clients worked in the mills a few minutes away. All but a few lived in houses around the corner, down the road. Their names were similar — Paddy and Peter, Mary and Rosemary — and in appearance, accent and demeanour they were almost indistinguishable. Same rough-cut suit jackets and tattered caps. Same worn shawls and frayed petticoats. Same tastes, too: beer and whiskey in the evenings, sherry and port on Saturday afternoons. Decent local people. Solid North and West Belfast folk.

But the world outside the pub wasn't so comforting. James lived in a society segregated along religious lines. A society dominated, moreover, by the majority religion, the majority ideology. Protestants made up sixty per cent of Northern Ireland's residents. Unionism was the official political doctrine of the parliament at Stormont, itself a devolved legislature created specifically to avoid union with the impending Irish Free State, to maintain ties with England. Historic Ulster contained nine counties, but only six were partitioned off in 1920. Catholic Donegal, Monaghan and Cavan were not invited. In the tally, their presence would have tipped the balance against Protestant ascendancy, towards equanimity.

More important, James lived in a very specific place in Northern Ireland. Belfast was the capital, the political centre, the industrial engine. Half a million people called it home. The religious split — 60/40 — seemed appropriate: as Belfast went, so went the Orange state. But there was a problem. Rural Ulster was sleepy and backward. Communities generally lived apart from each other and in isolation from everyone else. Small towns also tended to be safely segregated. Londonderry (later shortened to Derry) housed both Catholics and Protestants, but in handy division: one community on the west bank of the River Foyle, the other on the east bank.

Belfast, however, was more mixed. The River Lagan served as a partial divide. East Belfast, dominated by the Stormont parliament, was almost pure Protestant. South Belfast, though west of the river, remained largely Protestant, despite the fact that prosperous Catholics sometimes bought houses off its Malone Road. These areas were protected from unprosperous West Belfast by the Bog Meadows, a no man's land of muck and field, with the Blackstaff River, actually a stream, constituting the official border. Half the city, in other words, was like most other cities and towns in Northern Ireland. Half the city was a decent, safe place to live.

As a boy, James McNally knew little about that city. He was from the Crumlin Road, the traditional divide between North and West Belfast. His Belfast knew few tidy divisions. It consisted of two massive ghettos in the west — the Falls Road and the Shankill — and dozens of smaller enclaves, mostly in the lower northern suburbs. A few middle-class neighbourhoods were tentatively mixed; most were not. Nevertheless, these areas shared roads, walls or laneways with their neighbours. Schools emptied into the same streets. Churches faced off across intersections.

The Belfast James knew was an ordinance map wilfully misdrawn. Most of the demarcations on the page were irrelevant. To read the map, one had to hold it to a light that shone only in the north and west parts of the city. Then the true divisions would be revealed. The flashpoints and fault-lines, the walls and borders: they were all there, looming but invisible, defining but indiscernible, like family secrets. Map literacy was taught early in childhood. Adults, meanwhile, never stopped studying changes to the blueprint. The 1935 York Street riots were only the most recent example. After a week of pitched battles, beatings and murders, vigilante mobs succeeded in evicting five hundred families from a dockside neighbourhood. Once the families were out, a mixed area became an enclave; people who had felt reasonably comfortable in those streets no longer ventured down them after dark. The map had to be redrawn. Riots in 1920–22, 1886 and 1872, and 1864 had achieved similar results. The cartographer's invisible ink was rarely dry.

The key fault-line in James McNally's life ran right along the sidewalk outside the Mountainview. The middle part of the Crumlin Road was a flashpoint. Immediately behind the building loomed the Shankill. The boy had no business back there: not along Shankill Road, not even a block in from the pub. Gable-wall murals of King Billy made the point clear. The monarch perched atop his stallion in a red jacket, white breeches and a loomed blue or black hat. James had no business in King Billy's Glencairn farther up the street, or along the York Road back towards town. Certain parks he avoided. Certain shops he didn't go into.

But a block north of the Mountainview was Flax Street. It ran between Ewart's and Rosebank mills, and on overcast days seemed bowered in brick and stone. At the top of Flax Street stood the club James belonged to, the pitch where he played football, the terraced houses of friends from school. Along Flax Street and up Ardoyne Avenue were people who knew his mother, remembered his father, took a drink in the pub. People who knew his school crest and parish church, the colours of his club, the names of his older siblings. People who knew his face and name, or else, if they didn't know him personally, recognized in his looks and manner, even in his accent, something that was familiar and acceptable — something that belonged. They were right. James lived on the Shankill side of the Crumlin Road; he belonged in the Ardoyne.

But the Crumlin Road was still home. Homey, too: the rhythm of regulars stopping by for a pint; of workers filing into the mills at sunrise and pouring out at sunset; of the Farcet gurgling in a nearby ditch; of fishmongers pushing hand carts past the door, heavy with ice blocks and gleaming with herring from Lough Neagh; of coal carriages climbing up towards Legoniel, the carters dismounting on the steepest inclines.

Delivery carts also passed by the house of Maureen Daly. Their load was often ordinary — coal or milk, bread from nearby bakeries — but sometimes the horses sported purple pompadours and the vehicle was rimmed in black sash. The city cemetery was around the corner from the Dalys, on the slope of Black Mountain. Though intended to be mixed, the graveyard had wound up a predominantly Protestant resting-place in a predominantly Catholic neighbourhood. (Milltown, a kilometre farther west, was opened in the 1880s in response to pressure from the Catholic church to segregate burials.) Maureen and her friends liked to play in the massive grounds. The cemetery was close by and quiet, and had no bossy park keepers, like the Falls Park next door. Whenever a hearse passed through the gate, the kids hid behind tombstones to avoid seeming disrespectful.

Maureen had been born in a house on the Donegall Road in 1928. Below the Bog Meadows, the road was working class unionist. Up higher, however, especially near the junction with the Falls Road, the street became Catholic and, in spots, elegant. Protestant West Belfast was duly warned: SILENCE IS GOLDEN, IRA read the side of a gable wall facing down Donegall Road. Since Partition the organization, once the bold freedom fighters for a liberated Ireland, had been reduced to carrying out the odd raid and the rare political killing. The IRA's specialty had become demographics — specifically, expelling Protestants from Catholic neighbourhoods. As a child, Maureen watched carts piled high with furniture and clothing being pulled back down the road towards the bog. She was told the people were moving house. They were, but not voluntarily; after scrawled threats in their letter slots, bricks through their front windows. Purges often coincided with similar Protestant cleansings in neighbourhoods by the docks, along the various fault-lines.

The IRA had cause to be brazen on the Falls Road. The neighbourhood was an enormous, largely self-contained Catholic town. King Billy murals were scarce in these parts. Orange parades avoided marching along these thoroughfares. Turf was patrolled, territory was defended. During the Troubles of the 1920s, republican and loyalist gunmen had made incursions into each others' domains, and waged gun battles in crowded streets and back alleys. By the 1930s it was mostly boys, mostly squaring off in the Bog Meadows, mostly hurling rocks and insults across the Blackstaff. Still, Catholics wandered over to Shankill Road to shop. Protestants tended the graves of family in the city cemetery or attended services at a church above the Falls Park.

Daylight in West Belfast witnessed thousands of routine and peaceful tribal forays. Evenings, though, were less interdenominational — businesses were closed, pubs were local. Nights were sectarian. People slept where they should, where they were allowed.

Maureen was only faintly aware of these goings-on in the Upper Falls Road. Her world was one of black-soutaned priests and angelus bells, youth club outings and camogie matches. Neighbours around her went to the same schools. Neighbours around her went to the same mass. Front doors were always open and welcomes always extended. Her family was well established in the community. Like John McNally, Michael Daly had found success doing a job many Protestants found distasteful. He was a bookmaker, and worked for and among Protestants. He was also an avid golfer who later became the first Catholic president of his golf club. The bookie shop, however, was in the centre of town; the golf club was in South Belfast. Michael Daly was also a widower — his wife had died when Maureen was a child — with a house to run and six children to raise.

"A country is not worth the spilling of a single drop of blood," he would insist to his children. Maureen's older brothers did not wander down to the Bog Meadows to join in the sparring, and the IRA didn't bother recruiting from the Daly house. Family and faith, solidarity and devotion, ruled under that roof. But while the Daly kids might not be exposed to much bloodshed or tension in their neighbourhood, they did pass by streets of decrepit "two-up, two-downs", also called kitchen houses, every day. These residences, by far in the majority in the Falls Road, lacked heat and running water and indoor plumbing. Most housed families of five to ten children, a grandparent or two, an unemployed father. Maureen's favourite uncle lived a block away. His kitchen house had no alley. When the refuse cart passed, the outhouse bucket had to be brought through the hallway to the front door.

Every July 12, Maureen and her friends would hop a tram up into Andersonstown, then scamper down the slope to the meadows. The girls would watch the Orange parade unwind, weary but triumphant, into the Woodlands Playing Fields in Finaghy. They would observe the orange sashes and bunting, the bowler hats and gloves. They would wince at the cannon lambeg drums and shrill piping tunes: "The Queen" and "The Billy Boys", played for the umpteenth time that day. The march was supposed to be boastful and threatening. For kids who felt safe from it, though, it was fun to watch. The bog protected them from harm. Fear would keep the marchers away from their homes.

Over on the Crumlin Road, James McNally also observed marching bands descend the street. These lodges were on their way down to Carlisle Circus, where the main parade assembled in a sea of bunting outside the Orange Hall. For James, fifing whistles and lambeg thumpings signalled confinement; along with most Catholics in North Belfast, his family remained indoors for the day. Their neighbours and even customers were suddenly donning the uniforms of Protestant ascendancy. Their neighbours were about to swagger past the bar, stare rudely in the windows; they would soon be going red-faced trumpeting faith and state — their faith and their understanding of the state. Catholics had little choice but to close doors and draw curtains. Short of leaving town, there was no escaping Orange Day.

And unlike down south, where unemployment fuelled mass exile, the city kept most of its citizens. Jobs were out there, if you had the luck. There was always the army. Besides, people looked after their own. Belfast was a series of towns — villages, really. Everyone knew everyone else. Everyone had a cousin who once played football with your cousin; an uncle who served in France with your uncle. There were troubles, of course, a lot of bad business: some sleepless nights, some tragedy. But you just had to know your way around. Trust your gut. Trust your supports. Family was the obvious one: inside a house, you were always safe. Church was another. A city of spires: a city of faithful. It was hard to walk more than a few blocks without passing some house of worship. In most neighbourhoods, even the street you lived on would do. A few bad spots were the exception. The rule? Whole blocks of open doors. Invitations to call in any time. No need to ring first (who had a telephone?): simply walk through to the sitting room. Everyone was home, anyway.

"A cup of tea?"

"No, thanks," I answered.

"Coffee?"

"I'm fine."

"What about a sandwich or a scone?"

"Really. We had some —"

"A few biscuits?"

"Tea, please," I amended.

"The kettle's on," said Maureen, satisfied.

Bernie and Patricia entered the room. "Will I put on the kettle?" asked Bernie.

"Let me," said Patricia.

We were home from the pub. All the McNally kids, minus under-aged Ciaran, plus Pat and I, had gone off to a bar down the Antrim Road. It was a local, smoky and grotty, rank from spilled beer. Only Catholics drank there. Lots of Catholics, too: the place had been packed, bodies blocking the door, drowning the canned disco music. Sean had proclaimed the pub twice blown up. But not lately. Not in the last eighteen months. The bar was, in fact, one of the few still standing the length of the road. What a year 1979 had been in Belfast. What a decade, the seventies. In the grotty pub, we had learned more details about the seventies, about the year in Belfast, about the Antrim Road.

Pat had drunk pints. I hadn't.

Now, we set up in a tiny parlour off the kitchen. With no fire lit, the sitting room would be too cold; with nine of us squeezed into the small chamber, it would be cosy. James closed the door to the hallway. Ciaran arranged chairs along the walls. That left the centre open, as if for dancing. But Pat plunked himself down in the space. Good idea, said Sean. All the better to receive a bit of the stick. I had no idea what a bit of the stick was. Actually, even after two days in the house, I had only some idea of what the McNallys were saying. What they were saying was, however, clearly hilarious. They were all laughing — in bursts or rolls, into hands or sweater sleeves. Those not laughing outright were either recovering from a spasm or else allowing their smiles to spread, their eyes to brighten, in anticipation. Even Mairtin, the least expressive family member, seemed to be enjoying himself.

"Y'er man is full," he offered, indicating his florid Canadian cousin.

"Pole-axed," said Sean.

"Paraletic," offered Ciaran.

I had a question.

"I took strong drink," said Pat. "Repeatedly."

"No disagreement there," said James, standing in the kitchen doorway.

"He's stocious," said Sean.

"Steamboats," contributed Bernie.

"Fucking lockjawed," piped in Ciaran. He turned to Maureen: "Sorry, Mother."

"Puddled," said Maureen.

"Y'er man is punctured," concluded Mairtin.

I still had a question.

"Let's get a second opinion," said James, his cigarette a conductor's baton. "A fellow countryman might have more insight into Pat's condition. What do you say, Chuck?"

"Yea, Chuck Connors," intoned Sean.

Chuck was my name then. I wasn't happy about it, but I liked Charles even less. My father — a history buff who preached the villainy of imperial England, a republican who decried Canada's status within the Commonwealth, a citizen who considered bills bearing the queen's visage to be illicit tender — had nonetheless named his first son William Charles. In high school, uncomfortable with the old man's "Charlie," I declared myself Chuck, aware that it was both macho and faintly butch. The generic grunt of the North American male: bad as Kip, nearly as bad as Biff, Bud, Tip.

I glanced around the room. Bright, expectant faces stared back at me. Friendly people. Witty people. People expecting wit in return.

"Pat's pretty drunk," I managed.

There was a pause.

"You can do better," encouraged James.

"We're waiting," said Pat maliciously.

"Very drunk?. . . A wee drunk man?. . ."

Someone stuck a pin in a balloon. Pop! went the crack.

"Tch-tch," said Pat.

"I haven't got the language," I stammered.

"Who's for tea?" asked Maureen.

The parents served, first their guests, then their children. Besides tea, there were cakes and biscuits, ham sandwiches. Patricia and Bernie passed out plates. Sean poured drops of milk into cups. The pot wasn't fancy — stainless steel, the handle grimy — but kept liquid extremely hot. The cups, saucers and plates were of bone china. The parlour had a low ceiling and curtained windows. Though my fingers and toes stayed icy, I was soon perspiring. We remained in a circle, with James smoking in the doorway and Maureen shuffling to and from the kitchen. Pat was still the centrepoint. He had the trim frame of his male cousins, the coal-black hair of his female cousins, his aunt's full cheeks and doe eyes, some of his uncle's expressions. Mouth shut, standing still (North American men walk differently), Pat might have passed for a local. A Belfast lad. A Catholic Belfast lad, apparently.

"How can anyone tell?" I asked.

"You just can," answered Mairtin.

"You learn how to," added Patricia.

I was six feet tall, big-boned, with a long torso and broad shoulders. My nose and eyes, the tint of my hair; no feature was obviously Irish. Little need for me to drawl a few flat vowels or gambol a few paces for people from Cork to Belfast to ask: "What part of the States are you from?"

Oddly, though, that night I shared the periphery with the McNallys. I felt one of them, sort of, as they studied their Canadian cousin. Suddenly my friend seemed an interesting subject: the way he walked and talked, the way he thought about things. Suddenly I could see why the McNallys might want to interrogate, however circumspectly, a suburban Toronto teenager. It had never occurred to me that such a specimen might be of interest to a Belfast family, or to anyone else.

The thought was worth pursuing. I tried blending in even more.

"Who'll sing us a song?" asked James.

"Go on, Chuck," said Sean. "You've been quiet all night. Give us a Canadian song."

"A Canadian song?"

"Something you might sing at home," offered Patricia. "About the place where you come from."

"A Willowdale song," said Pat.

Willowdale was the Toronto suburb where he and I both lived. Where we "came from", I supposed, though I had never really thought of it in those terms.

"Let me think . . . ," I said, desperate to recall one of the French cradle songs my mother had sung to me. In the way, like a permanent eclipse of the sun, were the *de facto* melodies — the TV commercials and cartoon theme songs — of my youth. "There must be, umm, must be . . . ."

"Pat'll start you off," said Maureen.

"Go on, Paddy," said Sean.

"I'm fucking lockjawed," said Pat. He turned to his aunt: "Sorry, Mother."

That was funny.

"All the better," said Bernie.

The Willowdale lad rose to his feet. McNally irises further widened; McNally lips curved into smiles. An extraordinarily handsome family, I decided. Made all the more attractive by the humour and openness natural to their features. They were assuming the best. Anticipating wit and cheer from their guests — the proverbial crack. I, frankly, had lower expectations.

Pat owned a Wolfe Tones record. He sang:

> What did I have
> Said a fine old woman
> What did I have
> The Proud Old Woman did say
>
> I had four Green Fields
> Each one was a jewel
> But strangers came
> And tried to take them from me.

"Very nice," said James after a silence.

"Willowdale has a lot of green fields," I explained.

"Up the IRA!" said Pat.

"The Rah, you mean," corrected Sean.

"The lads," confirmed Pat.

No one glanced at Mairtin. He sat motionless, his head bowed, his arms folded across his chest. On his face was either no expression or else a studied neutrality.

"I'm pole-axed," apologized Pat.

"I think you're a wee drunk man," said Sean.

That was funny, too.

"Wait," I said, lightning-struck by wit. "I know a good one."

"Go on," said James.

I sang:

> *Pack up your Troubles*
> *In your old kit bag*
> *And smile . . . smile . . . smile . . . .*

Panicking, I scanned faces for signs of amusement. Expressions seemed frozen in shock, disbelief. My voice trailed off.

"Isn't that an English song?" asked Ciaran.

"It's a joke," I replied.

"Share it with us, Chuck," said Bernie.

I was too ashamed to explain the pun.

"Pat's pole-axed," I tried.

"Who's for a wee hot drop?" asked Maureen.

Hot drops of tea were poured. The biscuit plate was restocked. My T-shirt, buried under a collared shirt and sweater, was soaked; my ears burned with cold. I wanted a hot bath, a warm bed. But nobody else was moving. Worse, sweaters were being removed; sleeves were being rolled up. The room was "sweltering", claimed Sean. The kettle was back on, assured his father.

In the morning, Mairtin offered us a lift to the train station. He tried the engine, but without much hope; it had rained again during the night. Bernie took the wheel. Ciaran joined in and, with four men pushing, the Granada coasted towards the intersection. I got left behind. For the first time, the sky wasn't a ceiling. It was tall and blue and the clouds were fleecy. With the roof off, and the street running down, I suddenly noticed hills to the north and west of the neighbourhood. Actually, what I noticed were the slopes of hills so close by that their larger outlines remained hidden. Woods alternated with fields higher up. Summits were rounded and showed patches of exposed rock. Sheep could have wandered along the crowns. Cows could have grazed lower down. Lower down, however, were housing estates and shopping areas; were neighbourhoods; were North and West Belfast. Glancing ahead to the crossroads, I made still another discovery. The McNallys lived on a slope, too.

The engine caught just before the traffic light. I jogged down to the others.

"It's red," I said.

"It always is," answered Mairtin.

Ciaran stared at the King Billy mural. "Black pigs!" he muttered.

My gaze shifted up the intersecting street. What I saw nearly knocked me backwards. Due west was the profile of a mountain that consumed the landscape, like a cathedral in a village. The mountain had a sheer rock face and a jutting promontory. Its darkly wooded slopes were uninhabited. Its crown was starkly exposed. The transition from city to country, urban to rural, was as abrupt as a border: on the one side, houses and flats; on the other, forests and fields.

"What's that?" I asked.

"Cave Hill," answered Bernie.

Later, on the train to Dublin, Pat and I discussed what we thought we had learned. We had learned that the 1970s in Northern Ireland had been a disaster. We had learned that, so far, the year in Belfast had been a disaster as well. We had learned that life along the Antrim Road was shabby and gritty, not to mention tense, not to mention dangerous. We had learned that the danger, the shabbiness and grit, all had to do with oppression and inequality and history.

That was interesting. The McNallys were interesting. Beaten down by oppression, harmed by inequality, stuck in history. They drank a lot of tea. They ate a lot of fried foods. They talked unintelligibly.

"Do you think we could be interesting?" I asked my friend.

"To who?"

"The McNallys. Other people. What we eat and drink. How we talk."

"I doubt it."

So did I.

But another query lingered. Mairtin McNally, already in possession of the most idiomatic accent in the family, had left me tongue-tied with his routine greeting. "What about you, Chuck?" he would ask. By way of reply, I would try "Okay" or "Fine, thanks" or "Good." As answers, they sounded evasive. They made no sense. To be honest, I didn't know how to reply to Mairtin. I didn't know what his question was.

I kept this doubt to myself.

The border had to be near. After the disappointment of crossing in, I had high hopes: a wall trimmed in barbed wire, a tense security check of each passenger, a clearing of the car to scour for bombs. Within fifteen minutes of our leaving Belfast, the landscape had reverted to being an Irish postcard. County Down was possibly even more lovely. As we wound south through Tourist Board valleys and hills, my expectations diminished. When the train slowed on the outskirts of a town called Dundalk, I went through the motions with the conductor. Yes, Dundalk was in the Republic of Ireland. Yes, we had already left the North. Yes, I had missed the border again.

With our daughter strapped into the car seat and our rental Ford whizzing through the roundabouts of north Dublin, my wife and I resolved to quit worrying. Anna would be fine. We would be fine. In 1992, people in Belfast mostly shot people they knew, or knew of: targeted adversaries, selected citizens, former comrades. What about stray bullets? More likely, we reasoned, to be rear-ended by a truck or clipped by a drunk driver. Equally, in 1992 bombs in Belfast generally blew up the buildings and vehicles they were intended to: army barracks and police stations, the cars of enemies. The days of incinerating packed restaurants and crowded pubs were, for the most part, with the odd exception, over. Non-military targets were designated for maximum economic damage — courthouses and railway lines, supermarkets and government offices. Bombs planted near civilians were proceeded by warnings. Granted, sometimes the warnings were only fifteen minutes, or ten minutes, or no warnings at all. Granted, the occasional bomb detonated prematurely — in 1987, an IRA "accident" in the town of Enniskillen cost eight lives — often in the inept, trembling hands of its deliverer. Granted, the McNallys knew all about bombs, and people in London were quite familiar with explosions designed, more or less, to kill couples in rental cars with a child buckled safely in the back.

More likely to be hit on the head by a brick outside a construction site? More likely to be slammed by a bus while crossing the street?

Towards Drogheda and the ancient border of The Pale, I started thinking about history. Datelines popped into the head in Ireland as naturally as dividing lines appeared on the roads. Black spots indicating the site of a recent traffic accident blurred with black spots from the past: where a battle was lost, a rebellion was quelled. Forty country kilometres could take an hour to drive. That space might encompass counties and regions, accents and appearances; that space could be cluttered with decades of tension, centuries of upheaval. The sheer quantity of history could well have rendered it dim. But events from three centuries ago possessed remarkable powers of luminescence, if not clarity. Far from being distant, the seventeenth and eighteenth centuries in Ireland were right in your face: everyone studied them, talked about them.

A sign for Newgrange, a neolithic tomb, appeared near Slane. Down the road from prehistory stood the starting-point of the current chronology: the site of the Battle of the Boyne. King William versus deposed King James. Protestant England versus Catholic Ireland. The year of 1690: the conquest. No Surrender. We Remember. Drogheda, a few kilometres farther north of us, was a village of three thousand in 1649, when Oliver Cromwell ordered every occupant put to death. Catholics remembered that, too. Protestant planters recalled massacres of their kind around south Ulster until the Boyne proclaimed a victor, and a vanquished, in the war for Ireland. In Dundalk, a century after the conquest, the United Irishmen plotted to end British rule. Their rebellion failed in 1798. Dundalk, a half-hour farther north, still remained a refuge for subsequent plotting, fleeing and hiding republicans, especially since 1969.

The past in Ireland was united in fact, estranged in interpretation. It commanded attention the way a mountain in a city did: because of bulk and shadow; because of altered light, affected weather; because, whatever your personal views, you still had to negotiate with it — go over, go around, not go at all.

Where I came from, the landscape seemed unencumbered by such obstacles. My own background was presented to me as almost history-free. I was the son of an Ottawa native and a Franco-Ontarian. Though my father was the child of an army colonel and the grandchild of a senior civil servant in the Laurier government, he acted indifferent to his pedigree, removed from his past. Though he revered history, and possessed an encyclopedic knowledge of it, his interest didn't seem to extend to the offbeat or the anecdotal, let alone the private. We rarely went to Ottawa. I didn't know many relatives on his side of the family.

With my mother it was different. She was born in a small town in Northern Ontario. Blind River lay on the north shore of Lake Huron, between Sudbury and Sault Ste. Marie. Her father was a millworker. Her mother raised twelve children, all but one of them girls. The second youngest daughter, Muriel, recalled her grandparents only faintly. As for where her people came from, she wasn't sure. Maybe New Brunswick. Maybe New York State.

The town existed for the pulp and paper mill. Most towns up that far had just the one industry; if the mill or mine closed down, often so did the town. Houses were built of clapboard and inhabited by people who came from other places. This was the Canadian North. Roots didn't penetrate bedrock, crops couldn't grow without topsoil. Old meant the Depression; ancient meant the turn of the century. What was permanent was the woods. The woods went on forever. The woods never tired or lost ground. Humans huddled in temporary houses in makeshift towns until they ran out of copper or timber; until they ran out of support; until they had no more living descendants. The woods belonged. The humans didn't.

Most of my mother's sisters married local men and settled down in Blind River. One moved to Espanola, another to Sudbury. Only two Fallu girls left the region. My oldest aunt became a nun. Muriel met a twenty-one-year-old claims staker in 1954. This young man literally emerged from the bush; the previous winter, he had gone snow-blind staking claims around Lake Athabasca in northern Saskatchewan.

But, despite where the newlyweds met, the groom wasn't a local. He hailed from the nation's capital, six hours east by car. Moreover, after two years in Blind River, the couple decided to try their luck down south in Toronto. He found work in construction. She got pregnant. Soon after, they purchased a starter home in the suburb of Willowdale. Where all their roads ended. Where our family life began.

CHAPTER II

For all its pot-holes and black spots, there was only one road from Dublin to Belfast, and it was straight and narrow. Due north. Across the border. Into County Down. Deviation was often impossible; there was no other way. Nor was the main highway especially travel-friendly. Considering the links between the two cities, between the provinces of Ulster and Leinster, between Northern Ireland and the Republic, a wider, better-kept thoroughfare might have been expected. Roundabouts were far between: north Dublin, South Belfast. Drogheda didn't have a bypass, Dundalk had just installed a clumsy one. Towns had to be entered at the very bottom and exited at the very top. Trucks and tractors, bicyclists and pedestrians, all shared the same lane. Sheep crossed this road, too.

Most Canadian highways, in contrast, were ribbons: wide and smooth, unbroken. As a boy, I spent hours with my sister and brother in the back seat of the family Mercury. Outings included summer holidays in upstate New York and New England. The bulk of travel hours were incurred, however, during trips to Blind River. Before Highway 400 was built, the roads were all two-lane, packed with lumbering transports and law-abiding buses. My father stayed on Yonge Street until Barrie, then took Highway 12 to Coldwater and Highway 69 to Parry Sound. There the road turned to dirt until Sudbury, an exhausting stretch. At least the Trans-Canada to Blind River was paved; beyond the town, it reverted to gravel. The paving of roads, combined with the opening of Highway 400, halved the journey time.

Towns were well spaced up north: ten miles to Parry Sound, thirty-five to Sudbury. In between was a gas station and souvenir shop, a chip truck and motel. To pass the long afternoons, we sang songs and played car games. My brother and I counted Esso signs; my father quizzed us on the capitals of provinces and states, the names of presidents and prime ministers. On the older highways, towns still had to be driven through. We would glimpse a few outlying houses, front lawns of automobile shells and leaching rocks, then crawl along Main Street, past the Royal Bank and Steadmans department store, the hotel and railway station café; then a school, an OPP station, a few final houses. As the years went by, more and more towns could be avoided, saving time, maintaining visual continuity. Continuity consisted of ramps for logging roads and passes blasted from granite. Consisted of greens and greys; rocky fields and shallow lakes. Trees rimming woods. Woods fronted by trees.

My teachers called the landscape the Canadian Shield. TV shows referred to it as the hinterland. For my parents, for everyone from Northern Ontario, it was simply "the bush". My father could and did point out the various Indian nations that had lived in the areas: the rivers they used as transportation, the animals they hunted for food. But he seemed to be talking about the past, things gone, largely forgotten. The bush buried most traces, too. The bush did that to nations and communities, farms and enterprises. It didn't contain history; it obliterated history. One drove through nothing to get to something, to reach somewhere.

In summer these roads offered views of a deceptively tamed wilderness. Foliage was dense; fields rolled lazily; streams murmured in their beds. Irish immigrants arriving in May or June likened the Central Ontario landscapes to the countrysides of Donegal and Mayo. They immediately began clearing away the trees and rocks to build their homes, plant their crops. Summer vistas, though often monotone, were pretty enough. Not a bad landscape. Certainly nothing to be afraid of.

Family car trips in January were another matter. Those we took, we had to: to visit a sick aunt, to attend a funeral. They were, one and all, harrowing. Engines froze. Windows frosted over. Highways hadn't been ploughed, or were closed. Travel advisories battled radio static. Flashing oncoming lights warned of an accident ahead. My father adhered religiously to the rule of winter driving: keep six car spaces back in clear weather, ten spaces in a storm. He stored flares and blankets in the trunk.

In winter we were moving through a country where, even if we could read signs announcing Parry Sound in ten miles or Sudbury in thirty-five, we often had good reason to feel concerned and anxious, to wonder if we would find our way out of the storm, off the Shield.

I found my way back to Ireland in 1981. The first trip had been fun, if a little scary, especially the weekend in Belfast. I dined on it for ages. What a hellhole, I declared. What a disaster. I even had statistics: two thousand deaths in Northern Ireland in the first decade of the Troubles. Translated, that was thirty thousand Canadian fatalities in an undeclared, unofficial civil disturbance; for Americans, the figure was more like a quarter-million.

What was the problem? I was asked. The British, I answered. They were occupying the country. They were waging war. What was the solution? Brits out. Unification. Four Green Fields. Pack Up Your Troubles.

I heard Mairtin McNally's voice in my replies: the harsh consonants and drawled vowels. I heard his words, but not my own. Secretly, I had no words to offer. Secretly, I had no opinion to give.

But I didn't need words or an opinion at the Dunraven Arms Hotel in Adare, County Limerick. By late April 1981, I was the hotel's bartender, sharing a room in the staff wing. The Dunraven Arms was too good to be true. The hotel was two hundred years old. It had nine bedrooms, a restaurant, a lounge bar. Also a stable and a manicured garden. From the garden, one gazed at untilled fields and a twisting river. Out front was the highway — two lanes, no shoulders — known as the Tralee Road. Directly across from the hotel was the gate to Adare Manor. The manor was also too good to be true. Set on a leafy estate of eighty acres, the house was a genuine mansion, a proper gothic castle. The lord who occupied it was equally gothic: confined to a wheelchair, rumoured to be broke. Lord Dunraven drank in the bar. I served him whiskies "watered lightly". I watched other staff prostrate themselves before His Lordship, act servile in a way I had never encountered, and then mock the man afterwards in the staff room.

Hunters assembled outside the manor gate for a ceremonial glass of champagne. I served them as well. In my black trousers and white shirt; with my saunter and my accent. I got the assignment for purely physical reasons: being tall, I could easily hoist a tray of glasses to these mounted men and women wearing bowler hats and carrying riding crops.

A Norman castle nestled by the River Maigue. The castle was mossy and crumbled, with a tower that afforded views of the pastures and low hills of the midlands. Across a fairway — the ruin stood at the corner of a golf course — was a thirteenth-century church and abbey. The church floor was a mosaic of gravestones; the abbey courtyard sat waist-deep in wild flowers. In Adare was a thin-spired Church of Ireland and a fat-spired Catholic church. Thatched cottages lined the Tralee Road. The green was leafy and sheep-dotted; the village pubs were charming.

It was all too good to be true.

What thrilled me most, however, were my staffmates at the hotel. Now, these were the Irish I had heard about back in Canada, or more likely had read about in James Stephens' *The Crock of Gold* and watched in the John Ford film *The Quiet Man*. Named Timmy and Bridget, Noreen and Liam, with a half-dozen Pats and Marys, my co-workers were variously black-haired and blue-eyed, orange-haired and brown-eyed. They had high colour, especially in the cheeks and ears. They had freckles. Men boasted broad shoulders and hamhock thighs. Women possessed round faces and rounder figures. Tweed caps were common. Red wellies were still the fashion.

The Limerick accent was a delight. Breathless Cork patter met with measured Kerry drawl. Gentle to the ear, the accent nonetheless had to be learned. Vocabulary also required study. Staff used words like *gas* and *great gas*, *gas man* and *gas ticket*; they spoke of *codding*, *being codded*, a *codology*; they shouted *Ballocks!* and declared each other *gobshites* and *omadawns*. My boss in the bar, a wild man who downed pints of Harp lager after closing each night and then dragged me on harrowing moonlit rides to drink in *shebeens*, riffed on the word "fuck" — pronounced *feck* — like a jazz master: *feck, fecker, fecked; feck it all, for feck's sake*. These people were themselves *culchies*: country-folk, bumpkins to city dwellers. To me, they were authentic and funny and pleasingly odd. They had cinematic looks and stage-Irish accents and inhabited a prototypical landscape littered with German and American photographers.

The staff room was behind the kitchen. Though it featured a window onto the garden, a combination of grime, cigarette smoke and condensation rendered the chamber a cave. Staff preferred it that way. Furniture included four tables and a ratty couch; decoration was a television. Tables were regularly piled with teapots and dirty dishes, overflowing ashtrays, cups dotted with floating butts. The cement floor could be slippery: mashed french fries, runaway sausages. The daily *Irish Independent* was usually on hand, bloodied by ketchup, darkened by fat spittle, along with the *Limerick Leader* and the *Farmers Report*. Only two sections of these papers were sacred: the sports page, especially the sports scores and track results, and the entertainment page, mainly the TV listings and horoscopes. Other sections served as napkins, rags for shoeshines.

On the evening of May 5, 1981, the TV was humming and so was the staff room. I had been in there alone a few minutes earlier, watching the news. Bobby Sands had died during the night, and from the vantage point of Adare the footage of riots in Belfast, Derry and Dublin seemed preposterous. Sands had passed away in Long Kesh prison on the sixty-sixth day of his hunger strike. I had been employed at the hotel for only the final two weeks of his life, but his name had not once been mentioned in my presence, nor the names of the three other fasting republican prisoners. The H-Block protest, as it was being called, was having little impact on the Dunraven Arms. This silence went beyond the staff room; in the bar, where I now spent ten hours a day, conversation was concerned with local business — horses and football, the weather.

My news-watching was interrupted by the stampede of a dozen staffers into the room. The dining room had just closed, and waiters, busboys and kitchen help were finally being fed their tea. Plates of sausage and chips, egg and chips, beans and chips, were plunked onto tables. Pot lids clanged. Spoons rattled. Faces gazed up at the newscaster in puzzlement, impatience. I was about to provide the gruesome details when the assistant head-waiter, Timmy, climbed onto his chair and switched channels. "Dallas" was already fifteen minutes old. J.R. was acting evil. Bobby was acting good.

"Appalling," said Timmy.

"Outrageous," said someone else.

"It's a rerun," explained Mary the receptionist.

"But —" I said.

"No one blames you," said Timmy, a reedy man with a pinched face splotched in freckles and topped by a shock of orange hair. "You're a foreigner, and can't be expected to understand our ways."

"Shh, Timmy," said Bridget the dishwasher.

"Shut up, you."

"But Bobby Sands —" I said.

My boss, Mike Russell, leaned in the doorway. "Don't bother," he advised me. "Might as well talk to the fecking cows and fecking bloody sheep."

"Moo," said Mary the waitress.

"Baah," said Pat the sub-chef.

Mike Russell reminded me of someone. For weeks I couldn't put a finger on it. He had a Brillo pad for hair and coals for eyes. A handsome face had been swollen by beer and bad living. Sacks under the eyes looked bruised. A body, once thickly athletic, was now just thick, especially the soccer-ball paunch. Not that the extra weight slowed him down. Everything Mike did, he did with fury and haste, as if he was furious, in a hurry. The way he pulled pints and watered whiskies, sliced lemons and fixed sandwiches, was a source of amusement for regular customers, of alarm for strangers. The way he spoke, in sharp bursts, waving his arms like a man hailing a ship from a lifeboat, caused many to step back, keep their distance. He didn't smoke cigarettes; he sucked them. He didn't walk hallways; he stormed them. If the tap, tap of his shoe heels didn't send warnings, his muttered monologues did. He had worked at the hotel for a decade. He had lived in a Limerick City bedsitter for longer. He told me he was twenty-six. I'd figured him for forty.

Staff indifference towards the death of Bobby Sands didn't surprise me. Northern Ireland was treated as far away. (The border was about 220 kilometres due north.) My brief experience of Belfast elicited gasps in the staff room. No one else had been up there; no one had any intention of crossing the border. The border was, naturally, unacceptable. *Up there* was, of course, a part of Ireland. But what a violent part; what an alien, even foreign, part of the island. Full of bigots and terrorists; full of hard, humourless men and tough, sexless women. Waiters recounted tales of northerners, on their way to Kerry for a holiday, who had stopped in the restaurant for a meal. Taciturn people, one and all: tight with a smile, tighter with a pound. And their accents! Might as well have been Scotsmen. Might as well have been Welsh.

The group U2, now *they* were important. Everyone was listening to the new band from Dublin. Though their first hit, "I Will Follow", was already a year old, on hearing the song's distinctive opening notes on the kitchen radio the entire staff would explode into anarchic pogo dancing, especially during the chorus. "It's about God," Timmy explained.

The *Irish Times* filled me in on the riots, and later on Bobby Sands' funeral. There were murders and bombings in Belfast during the forty-eight hours following his death. For the funeral, the entire thirty thousand members of the security forces were placed on full alert, with six hundred special troops flown in to ensure the city didn't erupt. Some seven hundred foreign press scrambled for airplane seats, hotel rooms. IRA volunteers in black berets and masks fired commemorative volleys in the Lower Falls Road. A hundred thousand people observed the cortège climb the street towards Milltown. Millions more watched the funeral on televisions around the world. The honour guard and Irish flag, the oration at the open grave, the rioting that followed the dispersal of the crowd: it was dramatic and intense; it was the Troubles neatly summarized — a young man martyred for his convictions.

"He was a fecking edjit," said Mike. "They're all fecking edjits up there. Dying for their bloody country. For their Ireland. Well, sod their fecking bloody Ireland. It isn't mine. It shouldn't have to be mine."

We were behind the bar. It was midnight: the lights were dimmed, the door was locked. Mike was drawing himself a third pint of Harp. Beads of sweat dappled his brow. The perspiration wasn't from cleaning up, but from drinking so fast, so hard; from being so furious, in such a hurry.

Bobby Sands was five days in the grave. Another hunger striker, Francis Hughes, had just died. Two more prisoners were replacing them on the fast. Belfast, I gathered, was a genuine disaster: daily riots, nightly terror. A fourteen-year-old girl was killed by an army plastic bullet in West Belfast, and an eleven-year-old lay dying in a hospital by the same culprit. In the staff room of the Dunraven Arms, the evening news was being tolerated. Not watched, exactly, but at least left on. The front page of the *Irish Independent* was no longer used to wipe the tables. Headlines were glanced at; once I even caught Timmy reading an editorial.

"Sands was a wanker," continued Mike. "Have you even read a word about the man? Hopeless case, really. And his poetry? Fecking dross. They'll be reciting it in republican clubs around the country. They'll be singing miserable fecking songs to his memory."

He was right; posthumously, the twenty-eight-year-old Sands was emerging from media portraits as an affable but hapless revolutionary. Raised in North Belfast, Sands and his family were twice burned out of houses, and eventually settled in a West Belfast enclave. Sands got married at eighteen, was arrested six months after joining the IRA, and more or less spent the final decade of his life in Long Kesh. In prison, he found his true vocation as a political prisoner. He learned Irish. He wrote propaganda. He memorized Leon Uris's massive pot-boiler about Ireland, *Trinity*, then shouted the story down the corridors once cells were locked for the night. He practised Catholicism. He pencilled poems using the caged lark as a symbol.

While dying of starvation, Sands was elected a member of the Westminster parliament for Fermanagh-South Tyrone.

"He had a nice smile," I said feebly.

"Ah Jesus . . . ."

"Why don't you like him?"

"I just explained it. Francis Hughes, now, *he* was the real fecking ticket. He was a lad."

Francis Hughes stood in stark contrast with Sands. The notorious Hughes had been the most wanted man in Northern Ireland, a daring, ruthless paramilitary who operated in full combat gear and taunted the British by calling them up to say where he was, and then vanishing. As the strike started, he was serving multiple life sentences for murder, attempted murder, and causing an explosion. He was twenty-five when he died.

"Hughes scared me," I admitted.

"He was *supposed* to scare you."

"You admire Francis Hughes?"

"I'm fecking disgusted by Francis Hughes," corrected Mike, draining his glass. "I'm fecking disgusted by all those people. But at least he was what he was. At least no one can make Hughes into a hero after the fact. He lived a bastard; let him be that in death as well."

Two more strikers, Raymond McCreesh and Patsy O'Hara, died in late May. Four new prisoners joined the fast. Because of the pacing — a replacement was found only after a death — there was a lull in the convulsions. In the Republic, meanwhile, an election was called. Adare was suddenly filled with banners and signs, megaphoned orators stumping outside the Catholic church. It seemed a strange time to foist a campaign on the country. The two largest parties, the Fianna Fáil and Fine Gael, were both committed to a united Ireland. Fianna Fáil, the dominant party since 1922, embraced unification ardently, having enshrined it in the constitution. But their rhetoric was hollow. If the people I knew at the hotel were any indication, most southern Irish wanted nothing to do with the North, no part of unification if uniting meant union with the Troubles. (Which it did, obviously.) A united Ireland remained a metaphor for a future-tense state of happiness unrelated to any present-day circumstances or even to any felt past.

But the mood of the staff, like the mood of the country, was changing. Now the evening news was closely watched. Now the newspapers were being carefully read. Anecdotes concerning the dead men were common fare in the staff room and the bar. Everyone knew about the Sands family being chased from their homes when Bobby was a child. Everyone could tell you how old Patsy O'Hara was when he was first shot by the British. (He was twelve.) Timmy knew that hunger strikers Kieran Doherty and Paddy Agnew were running for the Irish parliament. (Both were elected; both died in July.) Mary and Pat could explain why Brendan McLaughlin had to be taken off the strike. (A perforated ulcer.) There were even Francis Hughes stories circulating, comic book in their excess and melodrama. Bridget liked those, especially. People drank in the bar with black ribbons — symbols of support for H-Block — pinned to their chests. They often sat beside customers whose lapels were coated in election buttons. Some people wore both. On a few occasions I heard raised voices; once a man shouted at a group at a table and then stormed from the room. He dropped his glass off at the bar on the way out.

The impulse to close ranks was powerful. Even in County Limerick, the collective enemy was abruptly Thatcher and the Brits, the Orange state. Even in Adare, the acts of a dozen desperate men were suddenly being clothed in the cloak of sacred history, of a holy past. Bobby Sands and Patrick Pearse, Patsy O'Hara and James Connolly. H-Block, 1981; Easter, 1916. Men dying for Ireland. Men dying to free others. Jesus Christ fit in there somewhere, too. Christ and the Catholic Church, the lark ascending, freedom fighters, liberty. It was confusing. Six weeks before, those same freedom fighters had been loathed paramilitaries and murderers; three weeks before, Northern Ireland had been a black hole not worth a thought, let alone a visit.

I felt the tug as well. The brutality of suicide by starvation was a factor; to read about the deterioration of these bodies — the fits and black-outs, the loss of bowel control — while eating lunch or sipping tea seemed grotesque. To read about the pleas of mothers and wives and children, the grief in nationalist neighbourhoods of Belfast and Derry, added an element of pathos and genuine tragedy. Everyone at the hotel was reading about the deaths, and watching TV, and growing more and more furious at British intransigence, the army occupation of the North, the Troubles; they were getting all worked up about imperialism, Partition, the execution of the leaders of the Easter Uprising, the failure of 1798, the Penal Laws, the conquest. And feeling weirdly guilty, I gathered. And Catholic. And Irish. And even Gaelic, whatever that meant.

Except Mike Russell. He wasn't buying it. Not a speech, not a sentence, not a word. One evening, he took on a half-dozen overnight politicos in the staff room. Mike was having his dinner. Actually, he was using his meal as a taunt, waving forkfuls of roast beef as he mocked and blasphemed.

"Eat your tea, Timmy," he scolded the waiter. "Go on, swallow another mouthful. Think it'll make a fecking bit of difference? Not to the IRA in Long Kesh and not to the starving children in Africa, either. Like your pretty black ribbon. Like your bleating about injustice and freedom."

"Don't get me going, Mike."

"Please . . . ."

"We have our beliefs," said Bridget. She was seventeen, sweet but scatter-brained. She was also a gab.

Mike didn't even deign to answer her.

Timmy did. "Shut up, Bridget," he said.

"Timmy!"

"You're all gobshites," summarized Mike. "You haven't a clue what the feck you're supporting. You haven't a belief in your heads. Six months ago, Belfast was on Mars. It will be back there again by this autumn. Here's where you live. Here's where you eat. So chew hard, lads and lasses. It'll stop up your mouths, if nothing else."

I made the mistake of smiling.

"And you," Mike said, pointing his fork my way. "Going on about your fecking friends in Belfast, how you're intending to see them next month. Are you hoping for a round of applause? A medal pinned to your chest?"

I stopped smiling. "I never said —"

"What are you going up there for, anyway?"

"To visit —"

"Poke around the garbage, is it? Study a world-class kip? Snap a few photos of dead milkmen, children killed by plastic bullets, coffins being trundled up the Falls Road? Maybe you can sell the pictures back home. Earn a few quid. Go on the telly yourself."

"Don't be mean to him," said Bridget, bravely. "He's just a Canadian."

At least three people told her to shut up.

"Gobshites," repeated Mike. "All of you. Canadian and Irish alike."

No one dared go near Mike Russell for hours afterwards. But later that evening, as we cleaned the bar together, he started in on me again. My impending trip to the North had been rubbing him wrong since I first mentioned it. In private, at least, his tone was softer; Mike was capable of displays of affection, even tenderness, as abrupt and fierce as his anger.

"What part of Belfast do your friends live in?"

"North of the city centre, I think."

"You think?"

"I was only there for a weekend."

"You want to be sure. Dead fecking sure, I'd say."

"They're Catholics, if that's what you mean."

"Ghetto Catholic?"

"Yes. No. I mean, I don't think so. They live up the Antrim Road. It's not like the Falls Road or the Shankill," I stumbled. "It's different."

He frowned. "Up the Antrim Road?" he said. "North Belfast?"

"Right."

"Ever heard of the Shankill Butchers?"

I shook my head.

"The Murder Miles?"

I shook my head.

"Ever occurred to you to do a little checking before wandering into a fecking war zone?"

I smiled weakly.

He groaned.

"Am I really a gobshite?" I asked, more to pronounce the word than to seek absolution.

"Less than the others," he answered. "But still too much. I keep thinking you should know better."

"Why?"

He shrugged.

We loaded the dishwasher.

"How come *you* know so much about Belfast?" I asked.

"I can read, unlike these other edjits. And listen, and take fecking note of things."

"You've never been in the North?"

"I've told you already."

"You don't sound like —"

"I live in fecking Limerick," said Mike. "You live in fecking Canada. Thank Christ for our good luck. Leave it at that, boy. Go to France instead. Go to Germany. Go *anyplace* but fecking Belfast."

I got it, finally.

"Why won't you visit Northern Ireland, Mike?" I asked.

"Because I'd end up shooting people," he answered, fixing his gaze on me. "Because I'd end up one of them."

I finally got something else, too. Though as physically dissimilar from Mairtin McNally as could be imagined, in the austerity and bluntness of his thinking, the disinclination to spare feelings, Mike Russell reminded me of him. Little wonder Mairtin had been on my mind so often lately.

I quit the hotel on July 9, the day after Joe McDonnell, the first of the second wave of strikers, died. I also called the McNallys. Except for a few letters from Bernie and an exchange of Christmas cards, I hadn't been in touch with the family in almost two years. But the invitation to visit was open, and an earlier call had been encouraging.

Maureen answered the phone. She was pleased to hear from me. I was welcome in their home. When I asked to come up that weekend, however, she hesitated. Getting an earful from her end, she passed the receiver to James.

"Marching season," said James.

I sort of knew what he meant.

"What with Joe McDonnell dying," he continued, "and the big Orange parade coming up, it might be wise to wait."

"Will there be trouble?"

"There already is."

"I promise I wouldn't —"

"A wee boy was shot dead in the Crumlin Road today," interrupted James. "A woman was killed last evening."

For some reason, I pushed. "Maybe if I just slipped in Monday or Tuesday, after the parade?"

"Why not wait a week?"

I agreed to wait a week. James handed the receiver to Bernie. She said hello. She said I was welcome. The same went for Patricia. Ciaran was out, but Mairtin was just coming down the stairs. Patricia passed him the phone. The pause lasted so long I wondered if the line had been cut.

"Mairtin?" I said.

The voice was soft and gentle, not at all like my boss at the hotel. "What about you, Chuck?" he asked.

On April 7, 1941, the German Luftwaffe launched its first raid on Belfast. The Republic of Ireland might be neutral, but the British province of Northern Ireland was not. For two years, the major yards had been busy repairing and converting ships for war, as well as building new vessels. Belfast's still formidable manufacturing engine had also been put to use: tanks, gun mountings and various aircraft parts were produced. The city seemed an obvious target for German bombs. Identity cards and gas masks, food rationing and air-raid drills, shelters and elaborate evacuation schemes kept even the most oblivious citizen from forgetting the existence of a deadly air war on the British mainland. Still, in 1939 Belfast had been outside the range of German bombers. By the summer of 1940 planes were capable of travelling the thousand miles round trip, but that required crossing over Britain twice; few experts believed the Luftwaffe would bother. In March 1941 the city had less than half the anti-aircraft cover necessary to defend itself; a few days before the first attack, some thousand mainlanders were evacuated *to* Belfast, for safety.

Six bombers flew high over the city that first night. After dropping flares to light up the docks area, the planes released successive rounds of incendiaries, explosives and parachute bombs. Harland and Wolff and the Alexandra Works were both hit. Errant bombs landed in East Belfast and along the Shore Road. One explosion in a flour mill claimed nine lives, but otherwise Belfast, now formally in the war, came through the attack well. Authorities hastily dispatched an anti-aircraft battery from England.

On Easter Tuesday, April 17, the sirens sounded again. The planes approached from the north-east, some two hundred in all, and swept low over the city. After an initial pass to drop flares, more bombers appeared. For five hours Belfast was pummelled with a ferocity unmatched by any other single bombing of a British city. While the targets were the same, the Luftwaffe actually did little damage to the shipyards and dock areas. Mistaking the Waterworks, a huge park-reservoir up the Antrim Road, for the lough, the Germans devastated swaths of North Belfast: York Street and Antrim Road, Cave Hill Road and Duncairn Gardens. The mill area of the Crumlin Road was bombarded. Ewart's Mill, Brookfield Mill and Edenderry Mill were all damaged; the York Street Mill, closer to town, was destroyed. Incendiaries and parachute-bombs levelled entire blocks in the city centre, wiping out neighbourhoods. There was less damage in West Belfast, though, and the south end was once again untouched.

Sixty people died when a bomb collapsed a shelter in the lower Shankill. After the York Street Mill was hit, one side of the building fell onto a row of mill houses, killing thirty-five. Belfast people died in shelters, in their houses, in the streets. They were killed by direct hits, disintegrating roofs and flying debris, fires. Bombs were huge this night, up to 250 kilograms, and destroyed multistorey buildings. The effect of those same incendiaries landing in neighbourhoods of detached dwellings, terrace homes and mill houses was terrible. One woman, watching servicemen battle fires in Duncairn Gardens, invited them into her house for a cup of tea. The building was hit, killing everyone in the kitchen. Nearby, a woman crouched under stairs with her two small boys. An explosion in the street fired a blast up her hallway. Though she still clung to them, both children died. The mother was unharmed.

Still virtually undefended, the city simply waited for the Germans to run out of bombs. The all-clear siren finally sounded shortly before dawn. Fires raged everywhere, especially in North Belfast, unstoppable because of fractures in water lines. Streets were bomb craters, cracked and split, or were littered with overturned cars and trams. Entire areas had no electricity or running water. Phone lines were downed. Some 900 people died on April 17 and another 1,500 were injured. Many bodies had to be dug out of houses; a few people, including children, were found alive. The city mortuary ran out of space, and corpses were stored in public baths and markets. The next weekend, a public funeral was held for 150 of the dead, all but 27 unidentified. The cortège wound through the city and up the Falls Road. Protestants and Catholics alike lined the streets to pay their respects. At the top of the road, corpses lacking rosary beads or religious medals were steered into the city cemetery. The rest, presumed Catholic, were buried farther up in Milltown.

Sixteen-year-old James McNally observed the air raid from inside the Mountainview. Armed with a hose and a bucket of sand, the teenager stood guard over the pub until his family finally took refuge in a shelter. Proximity to the mills ensured that the terror would be close at hand. James watched the mills burn and the sky flare red and white from explosions and fires. He smelled the gunpowder tang of magnesium. He tasted smoke. Next day he wandered down the Crumlin Road. The physical devastation was awesome, almost beyond imagining. Imprinted even more forcefully in his memory, though, was the sight of hundreds of destroyed houses and businesses, thousands of homeless people. Starting the next evening, James witnessed a nightly exodus of North and West Belfasters from the city up Divis Hill, to camp among the alder groves and gorse patches. The Crumlin Road funnelled this human traffic. In addition to the official relocation of some hundred thousand Belfast people to other parts of the province, for months afterwards terrified "ditchers", as they came to be called, piled their belongings onto the back of trucks, often onto carts, and marched past the pub to climb the steep road up beyond Legoniel, away from prospective bombing targets, intended or accidental. Next morning, bleary-eyed from sleeping in the open air, they marched back down.

Over in the Falls Road, Maureen Daly watched the April 21 public funeral file past. The girl, just thirteen, had spent the night of the first major attack in a shelter. No bombs fell anywhere near the shelter or the Daly house, though Maureen's older sister, a nurse at the Royal Victoria Hospital, did help defuse an incendiary that landed on the grounds. Michael Daly had little intention of either being stoic about another attack or sleeping up on Black Mountain. He hastily exiled Maureen to a boarding school in County Armagh, where she was safe but miserable — homesick for her family and the Falls.

The Luftwaffe returned in early May. This time, few residents watched the raid from their rooftops; few hid under stairways or beds; few assumed that being far away from a likely target meant their houses would be spared. More than 20,000 new shelters had been built in the intervening weeks. Anti-aircraft protection was doubled, and better fire-fighting equipment was available. Still, the Germans dropped their loads from higher up, more or less with impunity. Much of Belfast was set ablaze by 96,000 incendiary bombs, called the Fire Blitz. The harbour area was a sea of flames. Harland and Wolff, Short Brothers, the oil depot and aircraft factories were all massively damaged. Several corvettes were hit. A transport ship was sunk. Finally, after three tries, Belfast's war machine was put out of commission.

For James McNally, the Blitz was about destruction and displacement: property destroyed, lives ruined. Thankfully, the Mountainview was spared. The pub hadn't closed down and the family hadn't fled. Their home and business had survived the attacks. But other businesses, other houses, hadn't, and thousands of people had been driven from their neighourhoods. It was a sight implicit both of social disorder and of a loss of personal dignity that haunted him for years. There was one consolation, though; James assumed he would never witness the spectre again.

For Maureen Daly, the blitz taught a different lesson. Her father's determination to spare his daughter further exposure to danger, while infuriating to an adolescent, made a lasting impression. What a modicum of money and position could sometimes buy was simple escape, the opportunity to relocate. Commitments to community and business were all well and good, but not at any cost. The wisdom of saving your own, of getting out when things got bad, may have struck some as selfish. But it was wisdom still.

The war ended, and the McNally and Daly families prospered at their respective trades in their respective Belfast villages. Prosperity for city Catholics meant summers in the seaside village of Portrush, up the Antrim coast. Rented houses, days on the beach, evening teas and dancing in the local hotels; for the middle class, it was a season away from the war rubble and mill dust, the fife and drum of Orange marches. In a Portrush hotel James McNally met a daughter of a Falls Road businessman, and Maureen Daly met a member of a Crumlin Road publican family, a young man already known around town for his athletic skills.

The couple married in 1951.

Belfast was quiet then, still smarting from the Blitz, still grieving for its war dead. Its affluence as a manufacturing centre was on the wane: fewer contracts at the shipyards, less demand for expensive hand-produced linens. Harland and Wolff reduced its workforce, and mills up the Crumlin Road began to lay people off, even to shut down. In the centre of town, where power and affluence remained Church of Ireland, a play about sectarianism in the shipyards, *Over the Bridge*, caused a commotion. Otherwise, things were as they had always been. Leafy South Belfast was privileged and remote. Red-brick East Belfast housed a number of classes, but basically a single religion. In West and North Belfast people lived cheek by jowl; of course there was friction. But even the disturbances and riots of summer, usually along the Falls Road/Shankill divide, seemed routine. Tradition. The local sport.

If rioting was a sport enjoyed by Catholics and Protestants alike, it was just about the only one. In the Shankill, as in all of Protestant Belfast and unionist Ulster, the passion was soccer and rugby, the local Linfield club and the legendary Glasgow Rangers. (They played cricket at Queen's University.) The *Telegraph* and *News Letter* reported the scores, lionized the athletes; the BBC, on radio and later television, covered the action. But in the Falls Road and Andersonstown, as in Derry and Armagh, not to mention in the twenty-six counties of the Republic, the sports played were Gaelic football and hurling, and the athletes lauded in *The Irish News* — Protestant papers and the BBC ignored the GAA (Gaelic Athletic Association) — were footballers and hurlers. The Belfast Celtic Football Club, a soccer team made up almost entirely of Catholics, had flourished on the field for decades. Sectarian violence in the stands, however, doomed it; after a particularly nasty outing, directors disbanded the team and closed down the club.

James McNally played Gaelic football — for his local club, his school and eventually for County Antrim. He was fast, agile and strong, advantages in a sport that required huge measures of skill and toughness. Antrim was Northern Ireland champion in James's day, and their squad, composed of shopkeepers and bricklayers, students and the unemployed, were big men in their local pubs and churches, in the blocks and estates where they lived. Antrim footballers had status in nationalist Belfast. A man could be famous on one side of a street, be recognized by passersby, while remaining anonymous on the opposite sidewalk. A name could be legendary in one housing estate, be just another surname in the terrace around the corner. Even stature was sectarian.

This separateness applied especially to the GAA. For Protestants the organization was poisonous, more a Catholic fifth column than a sports club. They had a point. Begun in the 1880s in County Tipperary, the association had a mandate that transcended kicking a ball or waving a hurley stick. The original aim was to boost morale, purify race and religion, counter English cultural domination in Ireland. Both hurling and Gaelic football had been played on the island for centuries; Celtic heroes, apparently, enjoyed a good match. From the start, all but a handful of the participants were Catholics; all but a handful supported Home Rule. At nationalist rallies, bodyguards had used hurleys — ash sticks swung like bats on the field — to protect politicians. GAA men eventually *became* nationalist politicians — and prime ministers. Membership in the organization was pressing: anyone who played a GAA sport was forbidden to attend, let alone participate in, any "foreign" athletic events, including tennis or lawn bowling. Fanatics rooted out double-timers and the impure.

That was the pre-Partition, largely southern GAA. Things were different in Ulster. Catholics, a minority in the province but part of the overall majority in Ireland, were less aggressive about defending their race, promoting their culture. After 1920, their position was even further weakened: they were now just a minority. Opinions and ideologies were better kept to oneself. Kept for safe-keeping, almost: in kitchens and sitting rooms, local pubs and club lounges. Besides, most young men simply wanted to run around a pitch on Sunday afternoons, be with their mates, enjoy the sport on the field and the crack in the club afterwards. "Gaelic" was especially popular in Belfast. You didn't even need a playing-field; a ball could be hoofed around the road or in the alley. Gym teachers taught the basics in class; the priests were supportive (except at a few snobbish private schools), ever ready to explain how Irish, how Catholic, these fine games were. Fathers and grandfathers shared the enthusiasm. The GAA taught values beyond athletic skills. Teamwork, commitment, community. Continuity, too; with the rest of the island, with the past.

Games were played on Sunday afternoons. Sunday, in Protestant Ulster, was a day of rest. No shopping, no pubs, certainly no sports. The GAA highlighted Catholic blasphemy and nationalist disrespect. Besides, it was well known what went on in those clubs. Police raided them occasionally, and discovered not just republican posters and sentiments but republicans on the lam, weapons in storage.

James McNally emerged from this tradition. The sport was his passion, and the association formed part of his upbringing. His close friends were fellow players. He went on to coach youngsters. But these links were hardly constrictions. They hardly defined, never mind branded, him. After all, by the late 1950s he was equally a parent, a publican. James now ran the Mountainview. He and Maureen had young children. The clientele of the pub remained mixed, and though floorspace tended to be split along sectarian lines, he had a plan for the business that would make it over, challenge old divides.

He also had a plan for his family. Once there was money for a house, the McNallys might have been expected to buy in Ardoyne or back in the Falls Road. Instead, the couple went house-hunting up the Antrim Road, in lower North Belfast. Neighbourhoods higher along the street were gracious. Sidewalks were lined with lime trees. Ordinary houses were of red brick, and even in terraces featured arched doorways and round-headed windows, Ionic columns and ornamented cornices. Trams serviced the major arteries. The Waterworks was a fine park. There were schools close by, including James's alma mater, St. Malachy's; there was the Holy Family church on Somerton Road; and there were plans for more schools, a new church.

But when James and Maureen bought a house in Fortwilliam Park, it was not because the street was Catholic or Protestant. In part, they bought there because it was neither; largely mixed, largely middle class. They purchased a home near the bottom of Fortwilliam Park — once an exclusive Protestant area, guarded in spirit by elaborate stone gates at either end — because the middle and lower blocks offered attractive houses with easy access to the Antrim Road. True, a few mansions hid behind foliage along the north side of the road, and these were Protestant-owned. But the bishop had his official residence in Fortwilliam Park and, later, the city's only synagogue was built nearby.

Towards the York Road the street wasn't very mixed and, increasingly, wasn't very middle class. Beyond the gate, down near the dock areas, houses were "two-up, two-down" and attitudes were hard indeed. So York Road was best avoided. So were other roads, other neighbourhoods. And in Fortwilliam Park one was always friendly with neighbours, always polite, but also cautious. Where did the neighbour work? What schools did their children attend? Using a kind of Ulster code, James and Maureen could establish which neighbour was simply a neighbour, which might become a friend. Doors weren't automatically left open. Welcomes had to be extended carefully so as not to create awkwardness or give the wrong impression.

Using the Belfast map, meanwhile, the McNallys could also navigate the city's north end, happily reside within its labyrinth. Even Fortwilliam Park required a little creative cartography. The trick, taught early to the five children (the youngest, Ciaran, was born in 1963), was to think of the road as a cul-de-sac. Though it sloped down towards the lough, with houses clearly visible on both sides, in fact the street didn't extend more than a block to the east. An invisible wall closed off the rest of it. All the parents or children had to do was step from the front door and veer west, back to the Antrim Road. That was the direction of schools and church, shops and clubs, trams into the centre of town and buses up the Crumlin Road to the pub.

I was supposed to call the new house from the train station. That was made clear on the phone; ring, and someone would collect me. Orange Day was a week in the past. Another prisoner was dead — Martin Hurson, after forty-five days of fasting — and the British government was still refusing to enter direct discussions with hunger strikers. But the big news was out of Dublin. An H-Block demonstration trying to reach the British embassy had clashed with police, and 80 protesters and 120 guards had been injured. I had been hanging around the Irish capital until Belfast cooled. What I saw off St. Stephen's Green was nothing compared to the violence near the embassy in Ballsbridge, but it was plenty — marchers organized in three columns, seas of placards bearing the faces of dead prisoners, black ribbons. The protesters were not the usual student suspects; these were union men and women, labourers, the unemployed. Skinheads and toughs lingered behind the march to smash windshields and taunt police. It rained the whole afternoon; it was cold and grey; it was July in Ireland; the summer was being blighted.

James McNally had given explicit instructions. Even over a poor phone line, I hadn't mistaken his tone. But I had been waiting ten weeks to reach the North. I thought I was ready. After all, I had been in the hotel bar for arguments between customers. I had endured Mike Russell's sarcasm, challenged his doubting. In Dublin I had studied the determination of the marchers, the rage of the hooligans; I had experienced the tension of the march, the tight-fisted unease that was gripping the capital, the nation.

Besides, it was early Sunday afternoon. The new McNally address was in my pocket. All I had to do was walk through town, cut over to Carlisle Circus and proceed up the Antrim Road.

After asking directions in the station, I followed a street over to the shopping district. At the checkpoint, one RUC officer searched my bags while another performed a body search. The shops were closed and the roads were deserted. I heard church bells and the whoorl of a helicopter. I smelled coal. In front of the city library, back outside the security zone, I examined the posters affixed to every available wall and lamppost. I had seen a few of them in Adare, more in Limerick City, lots in Dublin. They showed the faces of the strikers. In terms of sheer numbers, Bobby Sands dominated, followed by the handsome Patsy O'Hara, the unsmiling Francis Hughes, plus the newly deceased — Martin Hurson and Joe McDonnell.

Hughes' expression was the exception. The other photos were of grinning young men with long hair and sideburns, wide-collared shirts. Hurson's photo appeared to have been taken at a wedding. Others might have been school portraits. They were, one and all, ordinary-looking Northern Irish men — local boys, lads. That wasn't surprising: Hughes might have been an explosives expert and Sands a theoretical revolutionary, but McDonnell had been an upholsterer from Andersonstown and Martin Hurson a welder from County Tyrone.

The posters were rain-blurred, covered up, defaced. They were also everywhere. I tried walking up Royal Avenue towards Donegall Street. The rain intensified. Two motor patrols rumbled by. Men stood at corners, holding their cigarette tips towards their palms, dragging hard. They kept their eyes down. At the same time, they watched me. I kept glancing at the posters of smiling dead men, the faces of unsmiling living men. I kept thinking I was sticking out, an uninvited guest at a party, a gatecrasher. I didn't feel afraid; I felt unwelcome. Finally, soaked to the skin, I entered a newsagent's for advice. He told me which bus to board.

There was a seat near the back. The window beside it kept fogging up. A few minutes into the ride, however, the glass stopped being an impediment to my sightseeing. Two panes, including the one beside my head, disintegrated. I was showered harmlessly with fragments, but the man next to me caught the projectile, a rock, in the cheek. He bled into a calmly produced handkerchief. The bus screeched to a halt and the driver rose to address his passengers. First he asked if the fellow was all right. Then he enquired if any of us had seen which way the "little fuckers" had gone. Information was volunteered: the little fuckers had cut through a vacant lot into an estate. The driver, a portly man already out of breath — from speaking, apparently — opened the door. Change in his pockets rattled like a tambourine as he took off.

The vacant lot, and the estate, were situated in a derelict neighbourhood. Ruins, some supported by braces, cosied up to houses with breeze-blocked doors and bricked-up windows. Spaces between buildings were often paved, littered with garbage and charred furniture, broken bricks and shards of glass. Less than a quarter of the houses along the road were occupied. Shops not boarded wore cages for protection. Lived-in houses had screens across their windows.

The air smelled of wet coal. The odour poured through the window frame. Soon enough, taunts from a gathering mob of kids poured in too: foul language spoken by grinning boys. Most of the abuse was hurled at the driver, who had just returned, wheezing and beet-red, from the war zone, minus the agitators. We applauded our hero nonetheless.

"Smash H-Block!" shouted a boy.

The bus jerked ahead.

"Up the Rah!"

The man with the handkerchief pressed to his cheek turned to me. His smile was curt. "Bloody Taigs," he said.

I nodded, anxious not to betray myself by speaking, anxious to be out of this horrible place, a neighbourhood, I assumed, that was far away from where the McNallys lived. Down by the docks, maybe. In the Lower Shankill.

A moment later the bus turned onto the Antrim Road. A minute later it stopped at an intersection, and I recognized the shops where James McNally bought his newspapers, the park — attached to the Waterworks — where I had gone for a walk with Bernie.

I disembarked.

The nearest phone booth was plastered on the inside with posters of dead republicans, on the outside with a poster of Margaret Thatcher, the words WANTED FOR MURDER printed below her collar. I dialed the

McNally number. James picked up on the first ring, and told me not to move. The Granada pulled up beside the booth two minutes later. Mairtin was behind the wheel. His handshake was punishing.

"What about you, Chuck?"

"Fine," I tried.

"You gave the parents a wee scare," he said.

"Sorry."

"But you're very welcome."

I thanked him.

"You're looking different."

"The beard," I answered. "Paramilitary trim. All the rage this summer."

"So it is," he agreed softly.

I closed the passenger door.

"And did you walk all the way out from the city centre?"

"Bus."

"Which one?"

"The one that cuts through a ruined neighbourhood. Back there a few blocks."

"Duncairn Gardens," provided Mairtin. "It's a flashpoint, you know. Tiger Bay on the north side is Protestant, New Lodge on the south is Catholic."

"They live across the road from each other?"

"Hopeless, really."

"Was it bombed during the war?"

"I believe so."

"Never rebuilt?"

"Aye. Then destroyed again."

Mairtin still hadn't restarted the engine. I had noticed that in Limerick: Irish people liked to chat in parked cars. Take a few minutes when a passenger got in or was about to get out. Once Mike Russell actually pulled off the road, the better to emphasize a point with his hands.

"Who were the Shankill Butchers?" I asked. Though my timing wasn't perfect, I was suddenly keen for details. And Mairtin seemed the right McNally to ask.

"A loyalist gang a few years back," he answered after a pause.

"They lifted Catholics off the streets and tortured and murdered them in the Shankill. More than twenty were killed."

"Which streets?"

"All over. The city centre and the Crumlin Road. Below us, too. Not far from here, I suppose."

"I see."

"They were caught two years ago, Chuck. Sent to prison. No need to worry."

"And Murder Mile — is it close by too?"

"Which one?"

I stuffed my hands under my armpits.

"They use the term for two stretches of road in North Belfast," said Mairtin. To my dismay, he shifted sideways and pointed. "The Antrim Road, from about here down to Carlisle Circus, and Cliftonville Road, which runs off the Antrim Road near Duncairn Gardens."

"We're on a Murder Mile?"

"It's just an expression."

"Describing . . . ?"

He blew air from his cheeks. Remembering the car tour, I was surprised by his reluctance. "This part of Belfast is popular with loyalist assassins," he said. "Neighbourhoods are either mixed, or else the nationalist areas are small and isolated. Easy to drive up the Antrim Road, shoot someone, then drive away. You can do the business and be back in your own house in a few minutes, having tea, watching the telly."

"People just select victims randomly and shoot?"

"Aye."

"How can they be sure they're shooting Catholics?"

"Mistakes are made."

"But —"

He started the engine. "I should get us home," he said. "The parents will be back to worrying."

"I thought this was a nice part of the city," I blurted, not expressing myself well.

"That's the whole point, Chuck. Middle-class Catholics, like Ma and Da, moved up here to escape the ghettos. The problem is, once you're out, you're exposed. You get a nice house, you know, but you also get burned by your neighbours, or else shot by strangers."

Mairtin headed north on the Antrim Road. He turned off after a short distance onto a leafy street of detached homes. Two more turns, and I spotted James waiting outside the front gate of a house. He waved and unlocked the gate, and Mairtin drove into a small driveway.

"Have I picked a bad time to visit?" I asked him.

"Depends on what you're after," he answered.

James opened the car door and pumped my hand. "You're most welcome," he told me. "Welcome in our house."

I had gifts: a cake for everyone, something special for Maureen.

"*Flahhrrs*," I said.

Ciaran insisted on carrying my bag upstairs. Patricia said I must be dying for a cup of tea. Maureen handed me towels. James instructed me to take the weight off my feet. In the sitting room, Martin was equally adamant that I sit before the mug of tea (unrequested) and plate of biscuits (ditto) that Bernie had brought in. A black dog called Aengus appeared. He reared, dropped his paws onto my thighs, then leaned in as if to lather my face. Bernie shooed Aengus away. Frisky, she called him.

"Great house," I kept saying.

"You're very welcome," they kept answering.

I still wasn't accustomed to hearing the word used that way. Where I came from, "you're welcome" was the bland rejoinder to a "thank you" often offered by rote. Now that I thought about it, to reply in such a manner seemed a little obsequious. (In my mother's language, the use of *bienvenu* after *merci* rang Anglicism bells. *De rien* — "it's nothing" — was the norm, though it sounded blunt. The formal *je vous en prie*, on the other hand, transported conversations to the court of Louis XIV.) Hearing the expression used simply, as in "You are welcome in our house, among us," was a revelation.

"God love you, Chuck," said Maureen as we sat for dinner. "Coming up here when things are so terrible."

"Sure, Chuck's anxious to see what's going on," said Mairtin. "Tell people back in Canada what the crack is. I'd say they're interested."

"I've been in Limerick since April."

"What about them?"

"Kids were wearing green berets and dark sunglasses to school," I answered cautiously. "People tied black garbage bags around lamp-posts. There were marches in Limerick City."

"The whole world is watching," said Mairtin.

James entered the dining room with a bottle of wine. "Limerick has outstanding hurling," he said. "They were all-Ireland finalists not long ago."

"People want to know," continued Mairtin. He stood in the door-way, his arms crossed. "Why are a dozen men starving in the H-Blocks? What are they protesting? What are the circumstances that have left them no other options?"

"The Gaelic is decent as well," said his father.

"In Long Kesh?" I asked.

"In Limerick."

"Some of the hotel staff played."

"What hotel?" asked Mairtin.

I hesitated.

"You'd hardly call the Kesh a hotel," he said.

"I meant —"

"Mind you, Limerick can't compare with Kerry," said James with some determination. "Finest footballers in the country down there."

"That was one of the reasons prisoners first went on the blanket six years ago," reasoned his son, with equal determination. "To protest the changes in status that made it difficult for republicans to learn Gaelic or study history. Language had a lot to do with it."

"I'm sure," I said.

Pop! went the cork.

"Now," said James.

The table had been laid for visiting royalty. A lacy linen cloth covered the surface. Atop it were patterned china plates and sterling cutlery, crystal water and wine goblets, a silver butter server and matching dishes. Also a decanter for water, a boat for gravy, a bucket for wine. Napkins had been ironed. The flowers in the vase were fresh-cut.

"I'd better go shave," I said.

"Wee bite of tea," said Mairtin. "Sit yourself down."

We started with cream of tomato soup. Steaks followed, swimming in a mushroom and red-wine sauce. On the warmed plates were also steaming potatoes and fried onions. Then came the accompaniments: carrots and green beans, tomato and cucumber salad, a mound of more potatoes. In one wicker basket was sliced brown bread, in another fresh rolls. I was plied with wine, lemon soda, water. I was implored to take second helpings. A bite of steak remained, a few onions, one more spud. I could find room, couldn't I?

Dessert consisted of poached pears with dollops of fresh whipped cream, chocolate biscuits, coffee and tea.

"Cream in your coffee?" asked Maureen.

"Why not," I replied.

James, the only smoker in the house, lit a cigarette. He had officiated at the meal with his customary authority. A slow, thoughtful eater, accumulating food on his fork (reversed, English style) and then pausing for minutes between mouthfuls, he was an unselfconsciously patrician man. Though he was now in his mid-fifties, his body and body language remained that of an athlete: trim and controlled, meticulous. He was certainly still handsome, with a wishbone face, globular blue eyes and salt-and-pepper hair slicked with oil. In motion his arms swung rhythmically, his stride was regular and smooth; at rest he held his teacup in mid-air, lost himself in the study of his cigarette tip.

The elder McNally was an extraordinary listener. Seemingly curious about everything, he would sit a guest down and tick off a pre-arranged list of questions, saying little himself, never tiring of the ramblings of others. His rapt attention was flattering; one felt important. But it could also be disconcerting. He was a person who looked directly, unwaveringly, at his conversation partner; I was someone who, stared at for more than a few seconds, assumed I had food in my beard. James would lock eyes, nod in encouragement, mouth *uh-huh*s and *that's right*s in accord. In some, the riveted look was a power play, a warning; in James McNally, it was a habit, an affirmation.

His laugh helped put people further at ease. James had a high, hearty laugh that emerged often, especially over the phone. He seemed to be always laughing, always making jokes, always enjoying the crack. He seemed always animated. For him, laughter, like good form, was a manifestation of politeness. His sense of decorum was strong. His sense of face was stringent. To maintain appearances, maintain cheer, was treated almost as a responsibility.

Never had I encountered someone who commandeered such automatic respect: of his family, of the friends who dropped by with a token gift of bread or cakes, of the shopkeeper who bundled a scroll of newspapers and a pack of Rothmans for him each morning. Of his journalist colleagues — besides running a pub in Armagh City, James covered Gaelic football for a local newspaper — at games. And definitely of the young Canadian he invited along to the shops, to the football stadiums, and who stood in frank awe of him.

After dinner we talked about Sean, now living in Dublin, and about what everyone else was doing: still studying, still working at the hospital, still operating the pub (without, I noticed, much enthusiasm). We also discussed Belfast, perhaps at its nadir that summer, with the city centre a mausoleum by sunset and the suburbs ghost towns after dark. Buses ran infrequently, especially in the enclaves; black taxis, operated by retired revolutionaries for paramilitary coffers, ruled the roads. Nobody went out at night anyway; though the Shankill Butchers were off the streets, other murderers lurked behind the wheels of cars and in the shadows of gable walls.

Indirectly, the conversation was about the strain implicit in living with the H-Block crisis. Directly, it was anecdotal. The new Catholic church on Cave Hill Road had been wrecked by a bomb before it was even completed; loyalists objected to it being built on "their" side of the street. While the church was now open, it remained double-locked — no casual visits with the Lord. Recently, James had walked down to the local police station to inform them that the McNally house would be empty for two weeks. When he arrived, he found the station blown up. No use talking with those people about security, he laughed.

Patricia told two anecdotes. She had been coming off a long shift in emergency one morning, and was tired and cranky. Noticing a soldier lining her up in the sights of his rifle, she astonished herself by crossing the Antrim Road to him. First she tried staring the young man down. Then, using her best scolding voice, she simply demanded that the teenager *please* point his weapon elsewhere.

Her second anecdote silenced the room. Patricia had been on duty the night Bobby Sands died. Outside the hospital, rioters battled police and army along the Crumlin Road, in New Lodge and Ardoyne. Towards dawn a father and son were brought in. The father was a milk-man from Tiger Bay who had set off at four a.m. to begin his route, accompanied by his fifteen-year-old boy. A Catholic mob tried stopping the van with bricks and rocks; the vehicle crashed on the Antrim Road and both occupants were crushed. The son was sent straight to an oper-ating theatre. The father was wheeled into emergency, where Patricia watched him die of head injuries. The boy died in surgery.

Dazed with fatigue and grief, she had stumbled up the cordoned-off road towards home. The lower Antrim Road was a mess: overturned garbage bins, looted shops, cars with their windshields smashed. Suddenly Patricia saw a stream of white liquid fanning down the street. The farther from its source, the wider the river, covering the glass and rubbish. Up ahead she came upon the milk van, still on its side, still oozing its contents after several hours.

We cleared the table.

"It's murder, plain and simple," said Mairtin. Only his father and I were left in the dining room. "Margaret Thatcher is responsible for the deaths of six men already, and there'll be more to come."

"She doesn't see it that way," said James.

"I couldn't care less what she sees, Father. Acceding to the prison-ers' demands would have been the easiest thing in the world to do. The conditions are only what we had in 1973, you know. She permitted the situation to escalate. She's committing murder."

"What do you think, Chuck?" asked James.

I was thinking about two things: Mairtin's reference to "we" prisoners, and his pronunciation of situation: *sit-ee-eh-shun*. After a two-year inter-val, I was back at square one with the Belfast accent.

"The prisoners are refusing to eat?" I began. "I mean, no one is actually withholding the food?"

"That's right," said James.

"Depends on how you look at it," said Mairtin.

"Isn't that more like suicide?" I asked. "Suicide for political reasons. In protest. But still . . . ."

James exhaled funnels of smoke from his nostrils. He nodded. Mairtin didn't blink.

"You said they were protesting?" he asked me. "Imagine a group of protesters carrying placards outside the Crumlin Jail. Suppose some peelers, or some Brits, open fire on them, killing several. Those people hardly committed suicide, did they?"

"No," I answered. "Of course not."

"Well then . . . ?"

I started to sweat. This wasn't like arguing with Mike Russell; not in this city, this house.

"Chuck may have a point," said James. "A man has to be responsible for his own actions. Sure, my getting shot by a soldier without provocation is hardly the same as my refusing to take food. In the one situation, something's done to me; in the other, I take the action myself."

"Governments kill citizens all the time without actually laying a finger on them," said Mairtin. "Bullets are a last recourse, Father."

"I don't think I follow."

Mairtin still didn't blink. He hesitated, though, staring down at his open palms. James, meanwhile, butted his cigarette. The silence wasn't comfortable. It contained other silences, I suspected: other conversations, some going back years. I had learned a new Ulster word recently, and it popped into my head: *thrawn*. Belfast, a book had informed me, had a "thrawn but estimable" citizenry. Not quite hubris, not exactly stubbornness, thrawn implied a pride of place that easily translated into excess pride, a reluctance to compromise. Belfast men, apparently, had thrawn in spades.

"Look," said Mairtin, "all I'm trying to tell Chuck is that prisoners are dying in the H-Blocks because of British intransigence. People are dying because the Brits are still here, and nothing is changing."

His "H", I noticed, was pronounced "haitch". His rhetoric, I noticed as well, was familiar. But Mairtin's words now sounded so alien I couldn't imagine returning to Canada and mouthing them, as I had before.

"I think I understand," I lied.

"Understand what?"

"What the strikers want," I said, sweating more.

"Go on."

"Peace, I guess. A chance to —"

"I wouldn't be so sure about that," interrupted Mairtin.

"Let Chuck finish," said James.

"The H-Block protesters want to be recognized as political prisoners lifted because of a political situation — the war in the six counties," said Mairtin. "Republicans want the British out of Ireland. Leave us to our own house."

"That's peace, is it?" said James tersely.

His son shrugged.

Why had I uttered that word?

"A lot of people haven't the stomach for the truth," said Mairtin in a quiet voice.

My eyes dropped.

"We'll have peace in this home, at least," said James.

I had a prepared statement: Choosing to fast until death *was* suicide, and people who bombed pubs and shot civilians were *not* political prisoners. What did I actually say?

"Thanks for dinner, James."

"Don't thank me," he replied. "It was all Maureen's doing."

I carried my coffee cup back to the kitchen. Mairtin followed me. In the hallway, I turned to him. "I think I'm a gobshite," I confessed.

He looked suitably perplexed.

I stayed with the McNallys for just three days that year. James brought me to a match in Armagh; Patricia and I went for a walk on Cave Hill. The mountain was a revelation, a wild, wooded place with a derelict castle along the lower face, a weave of overgrown paths ascending to the promontory, and a graffiti- and garbage-strewn crown. Up higher, accessible only by a hike around the summit, was a prehistoric fort.

Visible on clear mornings was the coast of Scotland. I saw no fort, no Scotland, but was still taken with Cave Hill.

I wandered the city alone. Rattling around in my brain was the list of neighbourhoods, streets and even blocks of streets Maureen kept nervously suggesting I avoid. (She didn't really want me going out at all.) The list was extensive; it was much of North and West Belfast; it was the places I most wished to see. I did stroll through the Falls Road and Shankill. I did return to the city centre via Sandy Row. But I was overwhelmed and increasingly addled. First by the hills that suddenly reared up to wall in the metropolitan area. How could I have spent a weekend here two years ago and only barely noticed them? South Belfast dissolved into the marshes and canals of the Lagan Valley. East Belfast was set against the smaller Castlereagh Hills. But the half of the city Mairtin had shown me that afternoon, the half I associated with the McNallys — these neighbourhoods were held tight by nature, like water in the palm of God's hand.

Equally overwhelming was the intensity of the propaganda/hate war being waged on the brick surfaces and gable walls I walked past. "Don't be Vague, Starve a Taig!" and "Four dead, saves us lead!" were memorable. Nationalist graffiti tended towards the declarative — "Smash H-Block!" and "Victory to the Blanketmen" — or else the hagiographic: "Blessed Are Those Who Hunger for Justice." Murals, a relatively new phenomenon in Catholic communities, were of notable artistry. Artists favoured larks trapped in barbed wire, hunger strikers depicted as angels, the crucified Christ. Drawings made from the poster faces of the prisoners adorned walls, along with lists of the dead and dying, taunts aimed at Margaret Thatcher and proverbs: "You can't put a rope around the neck of an idea." Protestant murals, less reactive (and less artistic), asserted centuries-old aims and allegiances: King Billys and Red Hands, Union Jacks and crowns.

The sky was leaden. The rain was constant. Belfast stank of burning coal and molten earth. Also of violence, more random than purposeful, and of death.

Inside the new McNally house was the scents of blooming garden flowers, the apple tang of furniture polish, a permanent coal camphor.

Inside the house were unrequested pots of tea and surprise water-bottles between blankets. Within the sitting room, where everyone gathered most evenings, was a stack of daily newspapers, a television permanently tuned to the news, a fire lit even in summer. In that room I could read the bad news, watch the horrors, from the comfort of a couch, in the company of my new friends.

But I hadn't come to Belfast to stay indoors. Unprepared for the city, inattentive to the McNallys, I suddenly wanted to leave. What about me? Mairtin was right. Never mind plastic bullets or starving republican prisoners; I wasn't even up for rocks tossed at buses, bombed churches, soldiers harassing tired nurses. (And I knew barely the half of it.) I hadn't the stomach for the truth.

And I presumed nothing would change. Taking little note of the fact that Sean McNally had already left the North, that Mairtin, unable to find employment, was talking about leaving, that Patricia was planning to study further in England and that Bernie was in her second year at the Polytechnic, I assumed the family was entrenched. I assumed a new house meant a renewed commitment. I presumed the McNallys would always be in Belfast and I presumed I would not be coming back.

When I returned to Ireland in early September, after a month on the Continent, the hunger strike was petering out. (The protest was called off a few weeks later.) Nine prisoners had been martyred so far, with some sixty nonstrikers, including many children, dead as a result of the disturbances. World media had already moved on, but the Irish Troubles, exiled to the News Digest column of most newspapers in recent years, were temporarily back in the headlines. Margaret Thatcher, ran the joke, had proved the best recruiter the IRA had ever had. Republican politics, until recently a fringe movement, were now mainstream. (Gerry Adams, a rising star in Sinn Fein, the political wing of the IRA, would go on to be elected Westminster MP for West Belfast.) Bobby Sands became the most famous paramilitary to kill no one but himself, and his choice of victim proved inspired. Winning by losing: an Irish equation that I couldn't solve, but that everyone else on the island, knowing their history, their Terence MacSwineys and Tom Ashes, could.

I called Mike Russell from the airport.

"I'm finished," he told me. "Quit the hotel, told everyone to kiss my arse, packed my bags."

"Where are you going?"

"The brother in Chicago."

"Why?"

"What a fecking question," replied Mike. I could almost see him waving his free hand. "Look around you, boy! Nothing here but dead bodies and black ribbons and old thinking, old doggerel. Nothing new. Nothing changing. I'm going where I can eat and drink and screw women. Feck everything else. Feck this miserable place."

"Good luck," I said.

"Maybe I'll run into you in the States."

"I live in Canada."

"Whatever."

Mary and I drove north towards Dundalk. Just south of the town was the hotel where, a decade before, Sean McNally and I had often stopped for a cup of coffee. After ninety minutes in the car, Sean had felt the need to break up the ride to Belfast. Ninety minutes was a daily commute for some crazed North Americans, but I had appreciated his sense of space. In a country where until recently people living thirty kilometres apart spoke with different accents, distances were elongated, space was expanded. If the accent of a farmer on the far side of a mountain slope was distinct from your own, most likely there were other differences too: the vocabulary he used, the source languages for certain of his words, even the music that shaped his ear. Bad roads had something to do with it. So did the lack of communication; electricity came late to many areas of rural Ireland. So, of course, did history. A farmer in Wexford spoke the way he did in 1992 because, in part, of the Norman invasion in 1169. Since the Normans failed to penetrate County Cork, however, the Cork farmer would more likely contain Elizabethan influences in his accent, along with some French and the enduring rhythms of Irish. In Ulster, a range of hills might separate a farmer whose ancestors were Scots and English planters from one whose ancestors were of Gaelic stock. In that case, a lot more than accent might divide them.

Even in a city, space required a different measurement. Where Sean McNally grew up, an estate across a reservoir or a field or even just a street housed people with a subtly but distinctly different accents. These people also had a different religion and school system, a different national allegiance and political agenda — also, apparently, a different look. Worse, they likely held antagonistic views of *your* religion and education system, your allegiances and agendas. They didn't care much for your appearance, either. Given all that, the housing estate was probably best thought of as far away: another city, another country.

The Dundalk bypass saved Mary and me from getting caught in street traffic. Over a bridge, past a graveyard, and the town was already in the rearview mirror. Ahead was a gentle countryside that ran into the Mourne Mountains, down to the Irish Sea. Tree copses were thick, hills were checkerboarded. Farms along the southern slope of the hills lay within the Republic; farms over the ridges, facing north, were part of The United Kingdom. A natural border, the mountains cloaked the actual 1920 boundary of Partition, making it undefendable, at times unlocatable — no border at all. Over a thousand roads and laneways bisected this infamous frontier. A handful had permanent checkpoints. Another few dozen were regularly patrolled. The rest were left alone — for the occasional paramilitary and smuggler, but mostly just for farmers and merchants, fishermen up at dawn and couples out for an evening drink.

As we entered a conifer forest called Ravensdale, Mary checked that our passports were handy and that Anna still slept. The road felt canopied by the woods. Ravensdale was dark and secluded; the trees were tall, blinkering. The wood, used in the past as a dumping ground for murder victims, had always made me uneasy. But I was no more comfortable with the army towers immediately visible at the other end. Planted into slopes like crops, the towers commanded a view of the licence plates of a vehicle emerging from Ravensdale even before it reached the border station. A money-changer and pub announced the official crossing-point. The station, though, looked abandoned. I slowed approaching the booth. Discovering it empty, its window glass cracked, I drove past the only remaining military border in the EU.

CHAPTER III

"CAUTION: AUTOMATIC RISING BOLLARDS" read the sign. Rising bollards? Laughter helped. Now we were waiting in line at a new permanent checkpoint a few kilometres inside the North. This crossing meant business: an island to segregate traffic, swivelling cameras and mirrors along the shoulder, a tower wedged above the road. Four soldiers aimed weapons at each approaching vehicle while an officer selected cars to inspect. To affect ease, I turned up the radio news. Reports from the former Yugoslavia dominated; the Security Council of the United Nations had just voted on a resolution authorizing "whatever means necessary" to deliver humanitarian aid to the people of Bosnia-Hercegovina.

Our turn came. The officer glanced first at the licence plate, then at my face. I stared straight ahead. With a flick of his left wrist, he waved us through.

"Token display," I assured Mary.

"Right."

"The army has to make it look like they're in control of the situation. Like they're doing something."

"Right."

"The border is porous. You can cross it almost anywhere. Why would a terrorist choose a road with a permanent checkpoint?"

"And rising bollards," she added.

Anna, now awake, spotted a field of sheep. We had invented a car game: if animals were sighted, one called out their sounds in conjunction with their names: moo-cow, baa-sheep and so on. The first to call was cheered. The last was booed. Cows and sheep were omnipresent. Dogs were frequent, cats less so. We saw chickens in Kerry. Anna was certain she glimpsed a bear in Cork. Of course, she also swore she witnessed a cow jump over the moon one night in Kilkenny. (*Goodnight Moon* was her favourite book.)

"Baa-sheep!" she now sang.

"Essssoo!" I had shouted as a boy. Counting gas stations had helped ease the boredom of the Blind River to Toronto drive. Our family lived ten miles east of the bottom of Highway 400, two miles north of the 401. Our house was on a freshly paved street in a recent neighbourhood in a postwar suburb. In the 1940s, Dunview Avenue was a field. In 1958, when my parents bought their home, there were meadows out back and to the west. (All of Toronto was flat: no mountains impeded views.) As demand grew, more houses were built and more fields disappeared. Homes weren't uniform in design, but were uniformly simple: brick bungalows and split-levels, clapboard storey-and-a-halves. Streets were laid out on a grid. For a long time, corner plots and connector roads remained open terrain, excellent for hide-and-seek, cowboys and Indians. Plots were narrow and outer walls almost touched, but residences were officially "detached". Space was what drew people so far north of the city. Space and cheap homes; space and recently paved streets, promises of sidewalks and parks. A shopping mall within walking distance. New schools. New churches.

The block contained a dozen houses on each side of the road. Our storey-and-a-half was the third from the top. Neighbours were plumbers and printers, mechanics and city workers, schoolteachers and CBC employees. They came from different cities and provinces and countries; they attended different churches; they sent their children to different schools. To a young boy, this seemed a diverse, eclectic mix, from all walks of life, all corners of the globe. These people took trips on airplanes and vacations abroad. Relatives visited from London and Auckland; a grandfather from Edinburgh moved into the spare room. Even our twice-monthly cleaning lady, who lived near Finch Avenue, contributed. Mrs. Giannini had emigrated from Sicily thirty years before. She had olive skin and wiry black hair. "Cleana you room," she would warn me in her lilting non-English. "Nice boy, Chalee. Go bye now. Nice boy."

All corners of the globe and all walks of life settled onto Dunview Avenue with apparent ease. First, everyone agreed to forget about the past. History was fine, so long as it remained associated with some-place else. Belonging to a different culture was fine, too. After all, suburbs like Willowdale didn't promote belonging; they promoted living — prosperous, anonymous living. So long as a sense of history or belonging didn't interfere, didn't complicate matters, it was okay. Just keep the nostalgia indoors. To yourself.

Remarkably, this even applied to things and sentiments Canadian. My father's insistence on pointing out where on Yonge Street William Lyon Mackenzie had led the 1837 revolt seemed mawkish, a little embarrassing. The same for his mandatory family excursions to Fort York and Pioneer Village. Flags didn't flap along our street until he erected a pole in the backyard. The first anthem I recall hearing, in a movie house, was "God Save the Queen". Two civic holidays stood out. Fireworks and general hoopla, courtesy of Buffalo TV stations, made the fourth of July unforgettable. And the 24th of May was the queen's birthday.

There were also the usual bonds of lifestyle and circumstance; lots of prams and playing kids, one-car driveways, dads mowing lawns on weekend mornings. The *Toronto Daily Star* slipped behind screen doors. The excitement over Expo and Neil Armstrong. Young families on a young street. White, middle-class suburban Toronto. But another, less obvious force proved equally unifying. At the top of the road, near the elbow with Longmore Avenue, stood a brown-brick housing estate. Not condominiums, not an old-age home. Government housing: subsidized shelter. Three houses from our own was the Willowtree Estate. The other Dunview Avenue community. The other crowd.

"You take the Catholic side," said Sean McNally. "I'll look after the other crowd."

"Does that make sense?"

"It does in a way, Chuck. I can do both parts, but you've spent too much time with the McNallys. You're nationalist Belfast, already."

"Thanks."

"I'm not sure it's a compliment."

But he laughed. November 1983, and Sean and I were driving up to Belfast for the weekend. I had been asking too many questions, seeking too many clarifications, making too many errors. Sean decided we needed a teaching tool. He improvised a car game.

"Start simple," he said. "You fucking Taig."

"Sorry?"

"Insults, Chuck."

"Prod."

"Fenian bastard."

"Black pig."

"Nice."

"Thanks, Sean."

"Call me Sammy."

"Sammy?"

"No Protestant would call himself Sean. John, maybe. Sammy sounds even better."

"I think of myself as nationalist, not Catholic," I said.

"I'm from good unionist stock."

"I'm a republican."

"I'm a loyalist."

"I'm Irish."

"I'm an Ulsterman. Not quite British, not quite Irish. A bit confused on that one, really."

"You're slipping out of character, Sean," I warned.

"Sammy to you, boy."

"I'm for a United Ireland."

"United Kingdom."

"I live in the North."

"The place is called Ulster."

"The Six Counties."

"What are you, IRA?"

"At least I'm not UDA."

"The UDA is a legal and legitimate political organization. You have a problem with that?"

"The UDA are participants in the war, aren't they?"

"What war?"

"The one the Brits are waging."

"You mean the security forces?"

"I mean the people responsible for the conflict."

"What conflict?"

"The Troubles."

"Ah those," said Sean. "We think of them as disturbances. Only in certain areas, too. Bad spots. Otherwise, Ulster is a lovely wee place to live."

"My cousins live in Derry," I said.

"Your cousins live in Londonderry."

"My uncle is in Long Kesh."

"Another Taig locked up in the Maze. Throw away the key, I say."

"England seems a million miles away."

"It's the mainland to us."

"The Republic, on the other hand, is just down the road."

"Ireland, you mean?"

"It's all Ireland."

"Is it?" said Sean, now well into his character. "I've never even been to this Ireland you say I live in. The wife went on a day shopping trip once in Dublin. Not me, though. Too many Catholics for my taste."

"But the island —"

"Was divided in 1690. King Billy. Battle of the Boyne. We remember. No surrender!" he added in his best Ian Paisley vibrato.

"Partition —"

"Partition only formalized divisions already thick on the ground."

"Segregation didn't create the hatred," I intoned. "Hatred created the segregation."

"Who said that?"

"One of my professors at UCD."

"A twenty-six county man?"

"A what?"

"A free-stater."

"Could be," I answered, getting lost.

"Is he a Dubliner?"

"Derry, actually."

"Which foot does he kick with?"

"Sorry?"

"Ah, Chuck," said Sean. "You disappoint me."

"I know the feeling."

"Is the fella Catholic or Protestant? Is he SDLP or Sinn Fein, UUP or DUP? John Hume or Gerry Adams; Molyneaux or Paisley? Does he play Gaelic or rugby? Does he cheer for Glasgow Celtic or the Rangers?"

"I'm impressed," I said, honestly.

"Don't be," answered Sean. "All bred in the bone." Then, as if to banish any bitterness from his voice: "Besides, it's good crack."

I lived in the Irish capital now, a graduate student at University College, Dublin. South-side Dublin was definitely not County Limerick. Doors had double locks; ground-floor windows were often covered by screens. The city had a crime problem, fuelled by a heroin problem, fuelled by a housing problem: too many dreadful council estates, too many slums. Dublin, I quickly realized, had a poverty problem. Ireland might be bucolic and lovely, but it was also near the bottom rung of the EEC income ladder. Rural poverty could be dressed up as modesty, quaintness. Inner-city poverty, especially in the narrow streets north of the Liffey, sported a neon sign: sloppy postwar apartment complexes, similar to those in the Falls Road and the Shankill.

Down on the south side, near the UCD campus and the posh suburbs, the concerns were different. A referendum on abortion had been held a few days before I arrived. The legality of the operation wasn't in question, but whether or not the constitution needed a "pro-life" amendment. Two-thirds of voters favoured declaring the Republic of Ireland constitutionally opposed to abortion. Debate during the months preceding the vote had been characterized, apparently, by hysteria and piety. The weeks and months following the decision featured despair among losers, and smugness among victors.

The referendum functioned as self-affirmation. Ultimately, it wasn't about abortion; it was about a psyche, a mindset. At issue was the desire among many southern Catholics to pretend away not only the twentieth century but, in part, the break-in problem in Dublin, the heroin problem, the poverty problem. Saying NO to abortion, like saying NO to divorce (in 1986) and to freely available contraception (until the late eighties), permitted the Republic to cherish a vision of itself as a pure Catholic nation, a warring Christian army. The fantasy was brutal. In 1983, Ireland was a no-divorce, no-abortion, no-premarital-sex, no-condoms, no-homosexuals nirvana, and anyone who said otherwise had to be a feminist, a pervert or just a godless socialist intellectual from Dublin.

I tried making jokes about this stuff with my new godless, feminist, perverted Dublin friends. We all attended lectures explaining the Irish psyche, the effects of post-colonialism, the bankruptcy of the nation-state model. Most of us agreed that the Republic of Ireland was a sectarian state driven by, among other things, an ideological agenda. Some used stronger language: it was a bullying theocracy, a priest-ridden backwater. A few were astonished by these revelations. One or two even disagreed.

A couple of friends braved the murky waters of unification. If southern social policies and attitudes were Catholic before they were compassionate or even logical, weren't Unionist fears of a United Ireland well grounded? Were the predictions of future-tense persecution mouthed by the likes of Ian Paisley really so hysterical? Wouldn't one pig-headed state mix with another pig-headed state like oil with water?

But these friends were in the minority. In Dublin I was meeting still another brand of Irish. These were, first of all, people who used words like *piss-artist* and *chancer*, *edjit* and *wanker*; who said *Howyis?* and spoke of *Your Man* and *Himself* and *Their Crowd*; who mispronounced Irish words, if they pronounced them at all, but also disparaged the neutral Dublin-4 accent and West Brit mindset; who, forced into coming up with an opinion about the North, muttered about the "barbarians" who murdered and the "sheer madness" that ruled.

These were urbanites, witty and sarcastic, detached. They read the *Irish Times* and the *Sunday Tribune* among Irish newspapers, and the *Guardian* and *Observer* among British ones. Unlike the West, where only the two RTE stations were available, their televisions picked up BBC 1 and 2, plus Channel 4 and Independent Television (ITV). They lived in flats off Harcourt Street and shared houses in Donnybrook and semi-detached homes in south-side suburbs, and were opera fanatics, movie buffs, vegetarians. They vacationed in Europe and talked about emigrating to London or the States. They had all been raised Catholics and were the products of Catholic schools. None of them was especially anti-clerical, but none went to mass either. Only a few had ever crossed the border at Ravensdale.

In some, uninterest in Northern Ireland was a stance: a gesture of defiance against the nationalism officially embraced by church and state. In others, it was a metaphorical assertion of the importance of the break-in/heroin/poverty problem, or of any one of a dozen neglected social and political concerns in Ireland. In a few, uninterest was a reflection of simple boredom, even disgust, with the North. On a personal level, the assertions were more complex and contradictory, possibly overstated for foreign ears. They weren't the Irish of cinematic ardour, real-life extremism; they got their politics from neither the pulpit nor the *Irish Press*; they felt perfectly whole, perfectly complete, in a partitioned Ireland. The North didn't haunt their dreams; they lived in Dublin, not Belfast; they lived in Europe, not colonial Ireland; they were sick to death of all that business; they reserved the right to care more about Düsseldorf than Derry, America than Armagh; they weren't like their parents.

Sean McNally had been in Dublin for almost four years. Though I hadn't seen him since 1979, on my arrival he immediately assumed duties first as host, then as friend. He called up to chat, extended invitations to dinners and in general allowed me to tag along with him around the city. His generosity shouldn't have come as a surprise. Already I had noticed James McNally in his son. Like his father, Sean considered good humour to be obligatory in himself, if not in others. He was always cheery; he was always solicitous and polite. Once, we had settled into a pub to await a friend. When she appeared with two strangers, Sean went into action: making introductions, ordering and paying for drinks, enquiring if everyone was all right. Putting these strangers at ease was of vital importance to him. Told that one man, named Michael, was from a non-descript midland town called Athlone, Sean fixed his father's gaze on him and said: "It must be quite interesting in Athlone, Michael?"

I asked him about this quality. As a teenager, Sean had worked weekends and holidays in the family pubs. My brief experience in Limerick had alerted me to certain less obvious duties of a bartender. Sociability, for example. Making conversation with customers. Listening to their stories. Showing interest and respect.

"I wouldn't know about that," he answered. Sean disliked talking about himself.

"But customers wanted to chat?"

"They did, of course."

"And you had to listen?"

"I never thought of it as a duty, Chuck."

"It was, wasn't it?"

He squirmed. "Part of the job, I suppose. But it was the crack, really. If it was good, you didn't mind."

"Was the crack usually good?"

"Most always," he laughed.

Sean's love of the crack was passionate. His vocabulary was crack-riddled. "What's the crack?" he would greet me. A successful night out meant "the crack was brilliant." "Are we on the crack?" suggested ongoing merriment. "I was just cracking" apologized for a jab, a harm-less taunt. While never as discombobulated as I was by Mairtin's "What about you?", I still took years to come up with a satisfactory response to Sean's greeting. "Just fine," I would usually reply.

Good crack demanded that everyone be relaxed. Good crack required witty conversation, lots of razzing, plenty of puns and silli-ness: a rhythm of sorts, more noticeable when it wasn't regular than when it was. Sometimes, good crack even required clowning. Sean had a boyish grin and a laugh so powerful it sometimes sent him rocking back in his chair. Naturally prone to offering the broadest joke, the clunkiest pun ("Chuck Connors" lasted for years), he found it no bother to laugh longest and loudest, to toss out the dumbest remarks, to encourage others to give him back a bit of the stick.

His personality seemed devoid of anger or ideology. He simply was not a Belfast hard man. He knew all about hard men, knew all about what the poet Seamus Heaney called "Northern reticence, the tight gag of place and times", and had even felt the steel in himself. As a child, Sean had assured his mother he was heading up Fortwilliam Park towards the Antrim Road. Instead, he had raced down to the shops along the Shore Road to exchange taunts, and often fisticuffs, with Protestant kids. High on fear and adrenalin, he had kept returning to the shops, kept lying to his parents. Once, Sean joined a crowd at an Ian Paisley rally barely a block below the house. The palpable hatred he felt that afternoon kept him away from further loyalist events. All through his childhood, and into his troubled high school years, Sean struggled with those responses in himself. They seemed at once alien and natural: part of him, but also imposed from outside. Meanwhile, the teenager grew more and more dismayed at the capacity of others in his hometown to exercise their fury and frustration with weapons, without remorse. Among the McNally children, he had gotten out of Belfast quickest, certain it was not a place he could live.

Sean was now twenty-six. He had a candid face, with an unfurrowed brow and permanently widened blue eyes. His hair was short and his chin was kept shaven. He sported black-rimmed glasses. Spectacles off, he squinted furiously until settling into the blankness of a startled deer. With the glasses on, he evinced a gentle, scholarly side, an impression at odds with piston legs that kept chairs tipped back, arms that kept crossing. The contrast was between restless movements and measured tones of speech; between a loose, gangly walk and a tight, athletic body; between a man who often consumed the better part of his meal while he was cooking it, and someone who could sit in a pub for an entire evening, rising only to fetch another round or use the toilets.

In the fall of 1983, Sean was selling office supplies. He had a part-ner, and together they peddled photocopiers, desks and chairs to busi-nesses around the city. Their office was a bedroom in the partner's house; their warehouse was the garage. The venture wasn't fly-by-night so much as fly-without-overhead-or-capital. I sometimes went along with Sean to help load chairs and unload bureaux. On these outings, it was difficult to tell whom clients treated more like an outsider. In Dublin my accent elicited indifference, or else the genial condescension extended to North Americans. Sean's tones literally alarmed many Dubliners; you could almost hear the bomb-squad sirens going off in their heads. Given that he was aspiring to do business with those same people, his partner's nasally local brogue proved important in convinc-ing clients that the company wasn't an IRA investment scheme. My presence during transactions only added to the confusion.

"Who's the Yank?" customers would ask.

"Canadian," Sean always corrected.

"The suburbs of America," I sometimes added.

The joke seemed appropriate. Sean's accent was often mistaken by southerners for that of Donegal, an Ulster county inside the Republic. For a moment he retained the status of ordinary Irish: Catholic, Gaelic, non-terrorist. Once his cadences and diphthongs were more precisely fixed, all that changed. He might still be a non-terrorist Catholic Gael, and the official position on northern nationalists was axiomatic — they were part of one big happy family — but he was also suddenly from Belfast. Worse, he was probably a ghetto Catholic, an oppressed Gael, a brother or mate of a terrorist. He probably had fierce politics, a stern gaze, a bitter tongue. He probably thought Dubliners/free-staters were all chancers and gobshites. He was probably a hard man.

Sean wasn't that way, but he was trapped, typecast; he was margin-alized. He was a child of colonialism. His identity had been blurred. Was he Irish, Ulster or English? Was he a compelling hybrid? Even his home wasn't really his home. "It's their town," Sean often said of Belfast. Home, for northern nationalists, remained an ideal. They were living in the wreckage of the British empire. They *were* empire wreck-age. For young people like Sean, education and the EEC allowed for escape, for renewed self-definition. Having been reared on the edge of England, shunted to the edge of Ireland, what other choice did he have? He wasn't a hard man; he was a post-colonial man.

I understood him, I explained during our ride up to Belfast, because I was post-colonial too. (I never missed a class at UCD.) Marginal because I was regularly mistaken for an American, regularly told there were no differences between Canadians and Americans, regularly informed (mostly *by* Americans) that the forty-ninth parallel was obsolete, a waste of cartographer's ink. Alienated because, though raised in a Toronto suburb, I grew up watching Buffalo news, humming "The Star-Spangled Banner", wondering why none of my friends' dads were fighting in Vietnam. Post-colonial because I was an Anglo-Canadian of French and Irish roots, by appearance more French than Irish, by education more Oxford than Harvard, by accent more Chicago than London; because I grew up in Marshall McLuhan's global village, and was an uncompelling hybrid; because, though I was a native of Toronto, the city had always felt to me like "their town" too, whoever "they" happened to be.

"But I'm Irish," Sean would reply.

"What about the border?"

"What about it?"

"Officially, it makes you —"

"Northern Irish."

"No doubts?"

"None whatsoever."

"Okay."

"I can even throw a few words of Gaelic at you. *Slan, Cathal. Conas ata tu?*"

"Sounds nice."

"My pronunciation is dire," he laughed.

"What about Belfast?"

"What about it?"

"It's not really your town, is it?"

"It's where I'm from."

"But —"

"Where my family are from. My mother's people. Da's parents came up from the countryside, of course."

"Do you feel at home there?"

"Not a question of how I feel," answered Sean. "Belfast just *is* my home. Good or bad."

"Oh."

"Would never live there, mind."

"And being Catholic?" I tried. "Even though you don't go to church?"

"It's on my birth certificate."

"Would you get married in a church?"

"No problem."

"Baptize your children?"

"No problem again."

I was silent.

"I do appreciate what you're saying about living on the edge, though," he admitted.

"Yes?" I said, hopefully.

"I'd always have preferred it if the house was lower down the Antrim Road. Closer to town, you know."

"Right."

"Know what I'm saying?"

"I think so."

Blue-eyed mischief? No doubt. My friend might be self-deprecating and modest, inclined to preface comments with "to my way of thinking" or "just an opinion, now", but he *had* opinions, had a way of thinking. In business he could be tough, even blunt, especially if he thought the other man was being less than forthright. On the football field he was both a natural striker — aggressive and smart, with an explosive first step — and a natural captain, willing to pass but also certain he could beat his tackle, advance on the goal for three points rather than kick it through the uprights. There was no arrogance in him, however, and no thrawn. Just a quiet confidence. An ease with himself.

Late on a Friday night, and we were already in Belfast, exiting the motorway at Clifton Street. Sean had turned up the radio: U2's

"Sunday Bloody Sunday", a song written to be an anthem, sung like a hymn and repeated on Irish radio with the regularity of a prayer. From the freeway, we crossed over to Carlisle Circus. Once an elegant circle, with churches and shops and a doctor's house ringing the roundabout, the circus was now largely derelict, one church closed, another due to be converted into rental spaces, and plots of land recently opened up by a wrecker's ball. A hold-over from an earlier era was the Orange Lodge, a stone High Victorian building surmounted by an equestrian King Billy statue, the monarch waving his sword in the direction of England, not Ireland. The lodge, adjacent to an off-ramp and therefore easily attacked, sported a wire cage that climbed up over the elegant central arch and second-floor windows. It still marked the rallying-point for the July 12 parade; the circus still constituted the foot of the two major North Belfast arteries, both leading up into warring enclaves and troubled mixed areas, wobbly middle-class neighbourhoods, mountains.

Sean negotiated the roundabout. He ignored the Crumlin Road exit, with both the hospital and jail just beyond, and entered the Antrim Road, due north towards Cave Hill.

"Home sweet home," he said.

I made him stop at the only shop, besides take-aways and off-licences, still open. He said there was no need; I disagreed. A moment later I returned from the newsagent with a bouquet of wilting flowers and a box of chocolates. We waited for an army patrol to pass by before pulling back into the northbound lane.

"Do you miss the city?" I asked.

"Not really."

"Too many bad memories?"

"Never mind the memories, Chuck. What's going on here and now is plenty to keep me away."

I nodded.

"I miss the crack, though," he added.

"With your family?"

"And my mates at school, and the club. It's not the same in Dublin."

His answer reminded me of something I had noticed on a previous trip: the closer we drew to the city and the house, the more terse became Sean's replies, the less frequent his jokes. He also began making a faint inhaling sound, as though he were sucking water at a fountain.

"This is a Murder Mile, isn't it?" I asked.

"Not according to the street signs."

"Did you used to walk along here?"

"Indeed."

"Were you nervous?"

"You always kept to the sidewalk facing traffic. Tried to study each car, check out who was driving. Once, a car pulled up beside me below the Waterworks very fast, screeching its tires. When the door swung open, I thought I was dead. It was just a mate. He thought he was having a bit of crack."

"Did you laugh?"

"I near hit him."

He sucked in air again.

"Were there more pubs back then?"

"I drank in a local that was located right across the road there," Sean answered. He pointed at a bricked-up building. "One night, a gunman walked in and sprayed the place with bullets. I was so jarred I fell to the floor. Wasn't hurt at all."

"Anybody?—"

"Luckily, no."

"Was the pub Catholic?"

"Indeed."

"What happened to it?"

"Blown up."

"Did your parents mind you drinking in a local?"

"I was maybe seventeen, and not into asking their permission. Things were quite dreadful then, you know. In Belfast, I mean. I took all kinds of chances, Chuck," said Sean, his voice quiet with astonishment. "Walking up and down the Antrim Road at night. Cutting through the Waterworks after dark. A bit crazy. Reckless."

I waited.

"Angry young man?" I finally asked.

"Something like that. With Mairtin lifted, and Bloody Sunday, and Internment . . . ." He shrugged.

"That's only the half of it?" I guessed.

We drove up past the gates to Fortwilliam Park. Cave Hill was a block of grey against a black backdrop. Even on a moonless night, the mountain remained an outline, a presence. I was anxious to reach the McNally house, anxious to greet James and Maureen in the hallway, to drink tea in the sitting room. I hoped there was a roaring fire. I hoped the doors were all properly closed.

The rain started up.

The Mountainview was destroyed by a mob the night of August 14, 1969. The bar the rioters burned down was not the same business James McNally had lived above as a child. He had remade the operation in the mid-1960s, and in so doing had challenged the orthodoxy of Belfast pub culture. In the city centre were establishments, like the Crown and the International, that paid little heed to sectarianism. Segregation was virtually unpractisable in town; all the people in the shops, restaurants and bars were out of their milieu. A man might drop by the Crown for a pint after work, read the newspaper and then catch a bus home. Likewise a couple or a group in a snug; no one knew their names or their parents, their estate or their church. No one knew which foot they kicked with. Even if they revealed themselves — say by reading the *Irish News* instead of the *Belfast Telegraph* — who would make anything of it, so far from home, so far from the neighbourhood? The city almost worked on neutral ground.

Downtown pubs offered anonymity and elegance, their Victorian interiors decorated with coloured glass and moulded tiles. Bars were of marble, snugs of wood. Some interiors boasted wooden columns, arcaded mirrors; others, dating back to the eighteenth century, had low ceilings, walls covered with liquor licences and city ordinances from the time of the Penal Laws. Many of these pubs served business lunches and afternoon teas, and employed cooks, waitresses.

Belfast locals were another story. Tucked into the enclaves and mixed areas ringing the centre of town, they tended to be unadorned. Older bars up the Falls Road and Crumlin Road might still retain tiled ceilings and carved wood, snugs for privacy and a lounge for women, but clients were indifferent to such charms. Locals were kept dim, day or night, the light amber and the air stained with wet towels and hops. No food was served. No music was played. Requesting ice in a drink drew frowns; requesting a beverage other than a pint or a whiskey was itself eccentric. Clientele, after all, rarely included men in suits or ladies with hats or Queen's students on a ramble. Clientele were workers who lined the counter, one foot on the runner, coils of cigarette smoke spiralling up to the ceiling. Clientele were old fellas in tweed jackets and caps, fathers with dole packets burning in their pockets, hard men whispering in snugs, the occasional group of women, the requisite drunk. Clientele had names and addresses (up around the corner: down the road), known backgrounds, known views. They went to your church. They'd gone to your school.

Sectarianism ruled outside the town centre. In the enclaves, bars could be counted on to service their crowd only. Who else would likely drop by? Mixed areas allowed pubs to coexist side by side; one served Protestants, the other Catholics. Proprietorship wasn't at issue. The problem was common ground; there wasn't any. Protestants wanted to drink among their own, to bring along grannies and kids, to greet the barman by name and be answered in kind. Catholics felt the same. Neutral pubs — true "public houses" as opposed to semi-private ones — were rare in North and West Belfast.

The Mountainview had always been a local with a difference. Not just because it was larger than most, with more varieties of beer on tap, a selection of fresh-cut sandwiches available and hot lunches prepared during the week. What really distinguished the pub was the mixing. Mill workers from both sides frequented the Mountainview. No one was unwelcome in James McNally's place. His *was* a public house. Still, being so far up the Crumlin Road reduced the potential drawing area to mostly Shankill and Ardoyne. Location was fact. Nor were allegiances, hard won, to be toyed with. Expectations had to be met.

James disagreed. He expanded the operation, converting the basement into a micro-brewery and the upstairs into a lounge. He hired musicians. He advertised in newspapers. He redesigned the interior, replacing the long bar with an in-the-round setup, positioned at the back. The plan opened up the floor without robbing the pub of the nooks and crannies certain customers coveted. Snugs still permitted privacy and, to the amusement of the family, Protestant and Catholic regulars somehow managed to stake out territories along either "side" of the circle. Newcomers, unaware of the clan lines, stood or sat wherever they could.

It worked. The pub began to draw customers from other parts of the city. Meanwhile, the old crowd hung on, albeit with some grumpiness at the influx of flashy, noisy outsiders. At the McNallys', the pints were first-rate, the staff was professional and the blend was, by suburban Belfast standards, unusual.

In part, James was being practical. Mills were reducing staff or else closing down, the machinery sold off to firms in Belgium and France. The Mountainview already looked out on a couple of abandoned buildings. There would be more empty shells to come. A wider client base might act as insurance against dwindling fortunes.

But he was also feeling optimistic. Belfast was no less bigoted a city in the 1960s, with double standards for Protestants and Catholics, systemic prejudice in housing and employment, and a habitual summer flaring of antipathies in hardcore areas. It was also a city lagging well behind other British urban centres in social legislation. Tempering these grievances was a mood — itself a reflection of the era — around town. Belfast was where a teenage Van Morrison, enamoured of American music, could find gigs for his first band. Where Seamus Heaney, up from the Derry countryside, could attend the once Protestant bastion of Queen's University and meet the like-minded, and begin to publish his poetry. Street life in the city centre was nocturnal. Sidewalks around the university were bustling after dark. Hotel lounges served sandwiches and tea until late in the evening.

Up in Fortwilliam Park, the McNallys lived next door to a French woman. The synagogue was around the corner; some of the new takeaway owners were Hong Kong Chinese, refugees from the high costs of London. Belfast even had a modest immigrant community, both scholars at Queen's and business people, outsiders who had few qualms about moving to a city formerly dubbed *une ville sanglante* by a French journalist, in reference to the red-brick houses and blood-red history. Certainly most locals saw little reason, barring another blitz, to seek exile.

James and Maureen felt the same way. No, things weren't perfect; no, the city wasn't exactly their own; no, change was hardly imminent. But much good was happening. James had inherited from his parents a modest structure. In the past, that inheritance might have come to nothing or, more likely, been taken away. Now, though, he — and his generation, perhaps — possessed the confidence to reinforce the structure's foundation, to brace walls, add floors. Mindful of the limited space and difficult location, James nonetheless pursued a program of cautious expansion. Not bad for a community that had always endured but only occasionally prospered. Prosperity now seemed imaginable.

Then came the 1968 civil rights movement. The marches and manifestos; the sit-ins in protest of housing inequalities and election gerrymandering. The crackdown by the security forces, the violent reaction by some Unionists. The riots. The provocations. The Reverend Ian Paisley, encouraging malice. The B-specials cracking heads. Then came Belfast's 1969 summer marching season. The usual boasting and bragging, but underpinned by insecurity and fear, bloody-mindedness and drink. The authorities professing to be in control, but in reality understaffed, disinclined to tussle with mobs, afraid even to venture into many areas.

Breaking into a newsagent's next door, the rioters used sledge-hammers to batter a hole through a shared wall with the Mountainview. James was inside the pub, as he had been every evening for the previous week, watching through a window as mobs roamed the Crumlin Road, firebombing businesses and burning out families. The night of August 14 was especially terrifying. Mobs were insane with hatred and alcohol. Armoured police vehicles drove up and down streets, firing randomly at looters and arsonists, anyone foolish enough to stray outdoors. The air cracked with gunfire; a pall of smoke — from burning houses — hung over the city.

Once the rioters were inside the building, James simply opened the front door onto the Crumlin Road. Within an hour his business was in flames; by dawn it lay in ruin. Some twenty other pubs were destroyed around town that night. "That was for James and the boys," bragged a loyalist pirate radio operator afterwards.

Also that night, James McNally saw the city through an eerie historical mirror. Entire families once again straggled along the road towards Divis Hill, their televisions, lamps and birdcages piled onto push-carts or the backs of lorries. Behind them were the homes they had been chased from by mobs, by their neighbours. The houses were located on mixed streets, in Protestant neighbourhoods, along fault-lines. The houses represented modest attempts at integration or, more accurately, indifference to enforcing segregation. Now the families were fleeing taunts and threats, fires and stonings, murders. Unlike Luftwaffe bombs, mobs could identify their enemy; almost all the forced marchers were Catholic. Equally unlike the Blitz, while most of the houses would be rebuilt, most of the businesses reopened, their original occupants would not be back.

Belfast's bizarre inner exodus, which saw more than eight thousand families harassed from their homes and neighbourhoods over the next four years, and was eventually described by a commission as the largest forced population movement in Europe since the Second World War, had begun.

Early in the afternoon of August 15, the Belfast Commissioner of Police asked the British to send in troops to help control the situation. The request was defended on the fancy that an IRA invasion from the Republic was imminent. At ground level, however, the truth was plain: the RUC and B-specials could not control the rampaging mobs. Troops arrived in West Belfast that same evening. Though hailed by terrified Catholics as protectors, the British failed to stop the expulsion of the residents of Bombay Street, or the incineration of houses along the Falls Road–Shankill divide. Calm was eventually restored, and a damage count was taken. Seven people had died in the disturbances. Some 750 were wounded, including 160 with gunshot wounds. Nearly 300 city businesses were damaged or destroyed, 80 per cent of them Catholic.

The current Troubles had been born.

James McNally had sent his wife and children to a holiday spot for marching season. On her return, Maureen found the business burned down and the city occupied by British soldiers. Rioting and vandalism had spread up to Fortwilliam Park, and the family next door was later firebombed. (Another neighbour was killed.) The McNally phone was ringing off the hook. "We're coming to get your da," threatened a voice to nine-year-old Bernie. "We're coming to get your da!" The girl ran screaming into her mother's arms. A family friend, a policeman, stood guard over the house that night.

The evening of August 16, after taking phone calls from a worried brother in England and a distressed sister in Canada, Maureen begged James to leave Belfast. She no longer wished to live in the city of her birth. She no longer wished her children to be raised in their hometown. Let's leave now, she said. Join Michael in London. Join Bernadette in Toronto.

James returned to the charred pub to tidy up and salvage what he could. Troops now lined the Crumlin Road to "defend" the vandalized businesses, and he chatted with the soldiers, who were friendly and courteous — a welcome sight after the recent madness. Though James dutifully turned up at work each morning for a few days, the Mountainview was unsalvageable. Being among the first material victims of the Troubles caused further hardship. A compensation system organized by the British government was hastily set up, but it was initially slow and complex, financially inadequate. In the short term, businessmen had no choice but to declare bankruptcy. The procedure might be routine, but for a proud and successful man like James McNally it was still a humiliation, a loss of face.

Other losses followed. As Catholics moved out in fear, the demographics of lower Fortwilliam Park began to shift. The new neighbours weren't so friendly. Doors were definitely closed; drapes stayed drawn in daylight. The block below the house, down towards York Road, seemed closer than before; some days, the Antrim Road was too far away for comfort. When the compensation cheque still didn't arrive, a decision had to be made. James and Maureen sold their house and moved into a flat in South Belfast. Home and business, both suddenly gone.

Aengus, I was assured, loved human beings; it was other dogs he couldn't stick. Neighbourhood dogs, for example, annoyed him to no end. Neighbourhood dogs were Taigs to be run off the street, Prods in need of a hiding. Around Cave Hill, Aengus was known to be a bully. He was known to wander, to chase dogs through open kitchen doors, into the paths of moving vehicles. He was known, moreover, to belong to the McNallys over on Leeson Avenue. McNally neighbours didn't appreciate having their spaniels and bassets and even their own Black Dogs of Belfast — the unofficial city mutt, part Alsatian, part collie — harassed. McNally neighbours were angry.

If dogs had worn tattoos, Aengus would have been painted with Red Hands and King Billys, Armalites and Che Guevaras. He had the wide chest of a bouncer, the solid torso of a boxer. His snout was a battering ram. His skull was a mallet. His wagging tail stung like a bee; once, a bruise welted up on my leg after Aengus whacked it. He weighed sixty pounds. His breath was meaty.

"Nice doggie," I always said.

"He's fond of you, Chuck," observed Maureen.

I came from cat people, and was accustomed to tight, ungenerous pet personalities. Aengus's slobbery, heart-on-the-sleeve temperament took some getting used to. He was indeed gentle with humans. His gestures of affection, though, were still abrasive: buckling my knees as he thundered past, driving his snout into my crotch on the couch. Even Quixote, the family tabby, was treated to rough love. The two had a quirky relationship. In the sitting room, Aengus would collapse on his side before the fire, with Quixote nestled against his girth. Nothing would happen for fifteen or twenty minutes. But then the dog would cock his head and, without warning, lather the cat with his thick pink tongue. Emerging from the wash, ears pinned back and whiskers dappled in drool, Quixote would expel an exasperated *purrt* and then wobble from the room. Hours later, Quixote could still be found in his kitchen basket, washing himself obsessively.

But tonight it was Aengus-the-bad who held sway. Sean and I were barely out of the car when Maureen, on the front step to greet us, admitted there was trouble.

"A neighbour called," she explained.

"Which neighbour?" asked Sean.

"Have a cup of tea first," said his mother, ignoring the question. "You both must be desperate for a wee drop."

"We'll get this over with first."

Maureen turned to me. "Quick cup, Chuck?"

I hesitated, being cold and hungry, longing for a roaring fire and a wee drop. Suddenly the air was seized by barks and grrrs and telltale yelps.

"Off you go," said Maureen, sighing.

I handed her the flowers and chocolates.

It was dusk. Higher up, the sky was dark; in the lower recesses, the hue was the colour of a bullet casing. Filaments of smoke hung over our heads. As Sean and I walked, Cave Hill kept appearing, then disappearing. Actual proximity was the obstacle; being so close to the mountain, a two-storey house succeeded in banishing it from sight. When that happened, the neighbourhood closed in on itself: too many buildings, too few trees. Then a yard or an intersection would expose the backdrop. The experience was akin to emerging from a fog in a rowboat and bumping up against a supertanker. From below, the mountain's conifer shoulders and basalt face looked remote from the city, aloof from city troubles. Winds blasted down the western slope. Birds wheeled over the rocks.

"Aengus!" I called.

Sean was silent.

"Don't you want to find him?"

"Those wee dogs can mind themselves," he answered. "I'm not their keeper."

"What about the family's reputation?"

"What reputation?"

"As the owners of a nasty dog."

"We don't know a lot of these people," said Sean, gesturing to the curtained windows and etched wood doors. "Families keep pretty much to themselves in this part of town. They're not actually neighbours, you know."

He walked with his hands stuffed in his pockets and his shoulders slouched. He also kept his gaze on the sidewalk, as if to avoid eye contact with strangers.

"You look suspicious," I had to admit.

"Our natural disposition."

At the corner stood a stately house next to a lot fronted by a long driveway. The problem with the house was that it had no roof or window glass; the problem with the lot was that it contained no house. Until recently, a home had filled the lot, inhabited by a judge and his family. Maureen McNally had heard the gunfire from several blocks away and dropped to her kitchen floor. The judge survived the assassination attempt, but moved elsewhere. The house was eventually razed and its neighbour, also damaged, was abandoned.

The shell reminded me of photos of houses in Normandy after the Allied invasion. Now, apparently, it was shelter for both vice-seeking teenagers and warring dogs. On a hunch, Sean headed straight for a crumbled wall behind the building. Sure enough, we heard more grrs.

I called the dog.

"Fuck yourselves!" came the non-canine answer from within the ruins.

"Must be my accent," I said.

Sean turned away.

"Aren't we looking for Aengus?" I asked.

"Aye," he answered. "And we found him, too, didn't we?"

His glasses had fogged over. Soaking wet, Sean seemed less suspicious, less — I suppose — Catholic. I resisted the urge to take him by the arm and lead him back to the house.

"What are we doing out here?" I asked instead.

Just then Aengus burst through a hole in the wall. The dog was in obvious pursuit; whom or what he was chasing remained unclear. Sean pronounced his name. Aengus stopped dead. With his bulging eyes and heaving sides, the foam ringing his mouth, the animal looked magnificent — straight out of Irish myth. I was mesmerized. Aengus returned my stare. Sean, head still lowered, kicked at the pavement. I thought to coax the dog home with promises of bones. His master had other plans.

"Go get 'em, boy," said Sean.

Once inside the house, towels hanging off our shoulders, we apologized for our dog-catching skills. I blamed Sean's fogged glasses, he blamed the falling dark. The table was set for evening tea. Mairtin was in London, finishing a graduate degree in engineering. Patricia was over in Glasgow, training in emergency medicine. That left just the parents, the two youngest children and the visitors from Dublin. A seventh party joined us between the appetizer and main course: Aengus, let in the back door by Maureen. The dog immediately disappeared under the table. Water jumped from glasses; silverware clanged on plates.

As usual, the meal was delicious: driven by meat and potato, doused in cream and butter, elegant in presentation. Despite Aengus, however, the atmosphere in the dining room remained sombre. Only afterwards, helping Bernie wash up, did I learn why. A bomb had gone off at the Polytechnic the week before, in a classroom full of RUC officers. Three policemen died, thirty-three more were injured. Bernie had been in the adjacent room. The blast had shaken the floor and ceiling, crumbled the shared wall. Except for ringing ears and a few cuts, she hadn't been hurt. None of her friends had been hurt either.

Sean entered the kitchen and put his arms around his sister. I took note of the gesture. Maureen joined us after a moment. She too embraced Bernie, who gave up trying to rinse pots and pans.

"Dear oh dear oh dear," said Maureen.

"Massive bomb," explained Sean. "The Provos meant business with this one."

"A lot of the survivors will be cripples," said Bernie. "It was really dreadful."

"Those poor men and women did nothing to deserve that."

"No one ever does, Ma," said Sean.

People set about preparing the house for the night. Maureen closed windows and drew curtains, flipped the lock on the front door but not the back — in case Aengus needed out. Bernie boiled water for tea. Sean refilled the coal bucket while his father stoked the fire. These activities portended a collective retirement to the sitting room for the evening. I hadn't given the family's domestic routine much thought, but tonight I decided that the sitting room was my favourite spot in the house and the evening my favourite time of day. I decided I liked the routines, the almost-rituals. I decided I wanted to help.

Maureen offered me door duty. Her assignment was only half serious; already I had a reputation around Ireland as someone incapable of closing doors. From Cork to Belfast, people were maniacs for shut doors and barred, blinded windows. For six months of the year, sitting rooms were often the only chamber inhabitable after sunset. Newer houses, like the semi-detached that Sean shared with two other men in south-side Dublin, had only the one fireplace. Older homes, like the McNallys', featured three or four hearths, but rarely were they all in use: too impractical, too expensive. The sitting room was the touchstone. Family members watched television there, read books and did homework, smoked and drank tea, brushed the dog and petted the cat.

Other rooms were arctic. Toilets were bracing, bedsheets were snow blankets. Breath turned to vapour in the kitchen (the stove provided some warmth); faucets emitted blasts of glacial runoff. Forget about an evening bath. Even if the immersion heater did fill a tub, even if the water was scalding, the air was so frigid that one ended up clean from the chest down, shivering into thin towels. The choice wound up being simple: the sitting room or else the local pub. From November to April, all other venues were unthinkable.

Of paramount importance to the cosy sitting room were correctly closed doors. Irish homes were far from draft-resistant. Windows were poorly set, doorframes were unfettered by straight lines or right angles. Even the keyholes in old doors, gaping as binocular lenses, funnelled breezes indoors. You could fly a flag in many Irish hallways. You could carve your initials in the frost on windowpanes.

At the McNallys', the door into the hallway was reinforced by a valance curtain and a wad of carpet stapled to the bottom. Together, they re-created a wall. The catch was the catch; the door could hermetically seal the room, reduce the rest of the house to a rumour, the ring of the kitchen telephone to a gurgle, only if the lock caught. I had trouble with this. I pulled the doorknob, heard the click, then moved on. Always there was a pause. Always it lasted just long enough for me to either sit back down on the couch or else disappear into the kitchen, before a mysterious wind, a phantom locksmith, popped the door back open.

Irish sitting rooms posed another challenge. While intimate, these often tiny chambers were also sweltering. No question of opening a door or window. No question of damping the fire; coal gathered heat, became more searing, as the night lengthened, especially when fuel was added to ensure cinders in the morning. Clothes weren't piled on as midnight came and went; they were torn off, folded onto couch arms or stuffed under chairs. Cold drinks weren't offered at one in the morning; another cup of tea was poured. I grew progressively more ruddy in Irish sitting rooms. I parted the curtains on windows, drew sketches on the fogged glass, rubbed fingers to my temples. Sweat trickled down my back. Thoughts curdled in my brain.

I also had to excuse myself. Teapots were being constantly refilled; nature had to take its course. Still, often I was the only person to rise in a two- or three-hour stretch, and slip out the door, and wait for the click, and hear the hinges creak as the crack widened.

"More tea?" asked Bernie that evening.

"Why not?"

"Know what I'm thinking?" said Maureen. "Chuck's sort of a funny name, isn't it?"

"Chuck Connors," said Sean.

"Woodchuck," said his mother.

"Chuckwagon," I obliged.

"Chuck Haughey," said Ciaran, referring to the Irish prime minister known more commonly as Charlie Haughey.

"Why do you call yourself that, anyway?" asked Bernie, one of her few contributions to the evening.

"It sounds less stupid in North America," I answered.

"I don't think the name is stupid," said James, mistaking my tone. "I quite like it, in fact. Simple and hard. Honest. A good footballer's name."

"Chuck's the GAA man, all right."

"Is that so?"

I sighed.

"The lads and me had him out to train the other day," continued Sean. He was now totally relaxed, North Belfast forgotten. "Chuck was a madman on the pitch. Never seen anyone bounce the ball like that. He was an inspiration to us all."

In Gaelic football, players could advance the ball down the field by either dribbling with their feet or else bouncing it off the turf while they ran. A rule limited the number of bounces, but as a novice I had considered myself exempt.

"I play basketball," I explained.

"Does the skill help?" asked James.

"He showed real promise," said Sean.

I had shown nothing of the sort. During the hour we practised, I had touched the ball precisely when, and for as long as, Sean and the others wished me to. They had dribbled and passed; I had slipped and fallen. They had kicked the ball between the uprights or into the net; I had squibbled the ball off the field, into the parking lot. They had been amused. I had been amusing.

"I lived in Quebec last summer," I said, rerouting the conversation. "Everyone there called me Charles." I rolled my *r*s: *Shharrrl*. "It was an improvement."

"*Shh-rrr-ull*," said Sean.

"We could call you Cathal," said Maureen. "Irish for Charles."

James lit a cigarette. He extinguished the match in his free hand with a deliberate, characteristic shaking motion: up and down, up and down. "You might not want your name changed for you," he said to me, going with the flow. "You might want to fight for it."

"I don't mind."

"Cathal's mother is French Canadian," said Maureen. "Isn't she?"

"*Oui, oui.*"

"It's all French to me," said Sean.

"I wouldn't be so quick to surrender Chuck," continued James. "You don't know what else they'll try taking from you."

"Speaking from experience, Da?"

"Don't get me started."

"You already are," said Ciaran.

"I'm only saying this: a man has to be on guard about everything in these times. They aren't just coming for your property and profession any more. It's your self-respect, even your name, that they're after."

"It's an exchange, James," said his wife, a little hastily. "One name for another. I wouldn't mind a new one myself."

"What'll we call you, Ma?"

"Anything you like, Bernie dear. Just not before ten o'clock in the morning."

"I think Sean should change his name," I said.

"To what?"

"Johnny," said Ciaran.

"John-boy," I offered.

"Sean-Phats to you punters," said Sean.

"Here it comes," warned Bernie.

"*Is dona linn an briseadh seo.*"

"What did he say?" I asked.

"We need Mairtin to translate," said Maureen.

"'We apologize for the breakdown in transmission,'" provided Ciaran.

Sean nearly fell off his chair from laughing. "*An bhfuil cead agam dul amach,*" he added.

"'Dogs must be kept on a leash?'" tried Bernie.

"'Can I please use the toilet?'" corrected Ciaran.

"Ah, you Gaels," I sighed.

"The name is McNally, thank you very much," said Maureen. She giggled into her teacup.

I had to excuse myself again. Tugging on the doorknob until it clicked, I let the hallway air cool my face. On my way back from the toilet, I heard a scratching sound. Tracing the noise to the kitchen, I joined Quixote, perched atop a stool, in staring at the back door. Briefly I considered retreating to the sitting room for advice. That seemed cowardly. I sought the switch for the back light. Not finding it, I simply turned the handle and let the intruder enter.

A creature stormed past me, buckling my left leg with his tail. He was gone before I could recover, and had taken Quixote with him. The dog was already lapping up Maureen's love when I reached the sitting room.

"How'd he get in?" I asked.

"Knocked the door down," said Ciaran.

"You hadn't shut it properly," said James quietly.

"But I —"

"Aengus does this trick to the knob with his nose," explained Sean.

I checked: my fingers were sticky. Despairing, I sank back into the couch. Aengus welcomed me with paws on my thighs, funnels of rank breath, a nuzzle of my crotch.

"Nice doggie," I said.

"He's fond of you, Cathal," said Maureen.

Later that same night, washing up once more in the kitchen, Maureen addressed less me than her city, her country. Her hands were fists. Her voice was an aggrieved whisper. "My lovely wee daughter was almost blown up last week," she said. "What am I supposed to do about that? What am I supposed to do?"

I was silent.

"Bernie's in a state," she added.

"I'm sorry."

"People at the Poly want her and her mates to see a counsellor. She went into the classroom," said Maureen. "A few seconds after the bomb went off, she went *into* the room where those people died . . ."

I wanted to ask.

"Two more to go," she added vaguely. "Then I'll sleep easily."

"Two more what?" I asked stupidly.

"I hope to God you don't raise your children in a place like this. Promise me you won't, Chuck or Cathal or whatever your name is."

"I don't have any children, Maureen."

"You will one day."

"I'm from Canada," I added, also stupidly.

"Promise me anyway."

"I promise not to raise my children in a place like this," I said.

"Thank you."

She put her hand on my arm. "What *is* your name, anyway?" she asked.

We both managed a laugh.

I met Bernie upstairs. She wore a nightgown and was carrying a steaming mug into her bedroom. Nonetheless, she immediately offered to fix me a cup.

"No more tea, thanks."

"It's coffee."

"This late?"

"Helps me sleep," she replied.

Bernie was a small woman with cropped black hair. Her eyes were dark, like Mairtin's, and she shared his hardscrabble accent. But her cadences were even more singsongy, with the upturned phrase endings, suggestive of a run-on question, of County Derry. I loved listening to her talk; I still didn't always understand her. But her laugh, explosive as Sean's, was infectious, and her smile beamed. We were the same age.

"I'm sorry, Bernie," I said.

"It was dreadful, so it was. I probably shouldn't have gone into that classroom. You think you might be able to help, but you really can't."

"Did you—?"

"Oh, aye. There were body bits everywhere. Arms and legs. Blood, too. Luckily, the smoke was so thick I saw barely the half of it, you know. Just as well."

"How did they get the bomb in?"

"It's dead easy," she replied. "The Poly is mixed. Catholics and Protestants, side by side. Supposed to be an example of non-sectarianism. That means anybody can plant a bomb and blow up anybody else."

She looked away. I said good-night.

"How's school in Dublin?" she asked.

"Largely theoretical," I answered, thinking out loud.

Bernie frowned.

"Fine," I amended.

I awoke early the next morning. James had already risen, eaten breakfast and returned to bed with tea and the newspapers. It being Saturday, the others would lie in. Throwing off the covers at dawn was not the local custom. Beds stoked at midnight with water bottles, swelled with blankets and comforters, remained cosy burrows until noon; by sunrise, corridors and kitchens, even sitting rooms, were wind-blasted fields. Drapes blocked out unwelcome light. Mutual agreement regarding movement ensured adequate calm. On weekends, the McNally household often did not stir, collectively, until towards lunch. The lie-in was sacred. The lie-in was law. Quixote slept in his basket all day. Even Aengus didn't dare cross his masters on this one.

I struggled with the schedule. Being an early riser, I often got dressed, descended the stairs and wandered the ground floor aimlessly before slinking back to my room and now frigid bed. I read. I gazed out the window at Cave Hill. I listened: to the house, to the sleeping. I also listened for the telltale augury of waking; a soft, unidentified knock on the door. The first time I heard the knock, I bounded from bed, swung open the door and stubbed my big toe against a mug of tea left in the hallway. Liquid darkened the orange carpet. The mug's handle snapped off. After that, with each knock, no matter the hour, I carefully checked the threshold. Though the tea suppliers sought anonymity, they were usually James or Patricia. Their knocks, designed to revive those lightly slumbering but not affect any still passed out, almost always lured sleepy residents to the door. Sighs would be appreciative; faint slurpings could be heard from back under the sheets.

This morning, I decided to give it a go. After all, it was nearly ten o'clock; how much longer could the McNallys sleep? (I had been up for three hours.) I dutifully boiled the water, selected a large stainless-steel pot from among the choice of vessels, dropped three bags in, filled it to the rim. A drop of milk — poured *before* the tea, as Sean always insisted — lightened the bottoms of six mugs arranged atop a tray. I allowed five minutes for the tea to steep. While waiting, I cleared a path: opened two doors, made certain Aengus was locked inside the sitting room. Then I carried the tray to the top of the landing. Like a mouse-catcher with his traps, I positioned the mugs outside the bedrooms. Only once each chamber had its cup did I move on to the knocking. I rapped once, soft but firm, on the doors. In length and crispness, two of the knocks were perfect. One was too timid. The other was too curt.

I waited.

Seated on the top steps, sipping from my own mug. Feeling satisfied; feeling pleased with myself.

Five minutes passed. Had I knocked too gently? Should I try again? Another five minutes crawled by. Steam no longer billowed from the mugs. My cup was lukewarm. Towards ten-thirty I quietly collected the cups, returned them to the tray, returned the tray to the kitchen. Each mug was washed and dried, reshelved. I was careful to empty the pot, cool it down with water, find its original spot in the cupboard. No one would notice a thing.

Aengus appeared so suddenly that I jumped. By my count, the dog had penetrated two closed doors. I retraced my steps. The door off the kitchen had been only partially closed. But the one to the sitting room was wide open; the inside knob was gummy.

The dog had interrupted my reveries. I was thinking about how welcome I felt in the McNally home. How happy, even safe, I felt here. How of late I wasn't as interested in reading the newspapers, watching the TV news, when I was in North Belfast as I was in Dublin or Toronto. How other priorities, other values, kept asserting themselves. How unexpected — and undeveloped — that thought was.

Christmas was only seven weeks away. Maureen had extended the invitation last night to share the holiday with them. I had accepted at once.

The dog wanted out. He whimpered, thumped the floor with his tail. Should I unleash the neighbourhood terror? He whimpered louder. His gaze settled on my crotch. I made for the door behind the kitchen. I turned the key, left in the lock, and tugged.

The cement porch was rain-stained. The sky was mud, the promontory smoky. Maureen's garden, left for winter, looked ravaged. Her apple tree was shorn of leaves.

Aengus shot out and rounded the corner onto the driveway. His claws went click, click on the asphalt.

"Go get 'em, boy," I said.

The Willowtree Estate was built a few years after our family moved onto Dunview Avenue. Land was disappearing all around our house:

our back yard no longer dissolved into a meadow; the Northtown Shopping Centre, over on Yonge Street, ceased to be visible from our front lawn. My parents were accepting of the changes. More houses and streets, more shops and churches, schools and hockey rinks; these were signs of progress, of prosperity. Developers had little fear of building on speculation in Willowdale. Astute businesses rented spaces in empty strip malls, at desolate intersections, with confidence that the mall would soon be fully leased, the intersection surrounded by houses. The Willowtree, financed by private enterprise, may have been a slight disappointment — the units were small, the lots cramped — but the type of tenant was acceptable. These people had paid good money for their places, or else were writing solid monthly rent cheques. They had lifer jobs, new cars, young children.

Then the government bought the estate and converted it into Ontario Housing. Ratepayer meetings were held, politicians made promises, but the sale still went through. Some tenants moved out immediately. Most stayed on.

When I first returned from Belfast in 1979, I realized why the city's council housing had seemed so familiar. The Willowtree had a Falls Road look: blocks of narrow dwellings — two-ups, two-downs, more or less — with postage-stamp gardens and no balconies. Windows were often boarded, walls were sometimes graffitied. As in the Divis Flats, front entrances and sitting rooms in the Willowtree didn't face outwards, towards the street, but inwards to courtyards and parking lots. Residents stared at each other. Outsiders saw only back windows and yards. Residents disappeared up collective paths and through the doors of buildings housing twenty, thirty families. Outsiders rarely saw them enter or exit individual apartments.

Bad things were rumoured to be happening thirty yards from our house: alcoholism and wife abuse, drug deals (in the late seventies friends snuck over to buy pot and hash), petty theft, gangs. We read about some of these problems in the *Willowdale Mirror*, once or twice in the *Toronto Star*. Mostly, though, we heard stories. In the evenings a police vehicle sat at the top of the street, engine idling, officers sipping coffees. Night-time foot patrols were routine. I remember halting a game of catch to watch

104 • CHARLES FORAN

a teenager be arrested. Mrs. Hill, unlucky owner of the corner plot, had her windows broken, her flowers uprooted. Shots were apparently once fired inside the estate, though no one heard them.

I wasn't encouraged to go into the Willowtree. None of the kids on Dunview Avenue were encouraged. It was an infected pool, and we were bathers cautiously circling the rim. Parents had concrete grievances against the project; Mrs. Hill's windows and garden, loud music on summer nights, Camaros dragging up the street heedless of kids playing hopscotch and ball. Some neighbours also had more abstract complaints. Property values had been affected. The rate of break-ins was higher on our block than elsewhere. (One Willowtree boy was caught.) A nice, quiet neighbourhood now had to make room for a government-created ghetto, we complained. Worse, we had no choice in the matter. We had to put up with it.

Our house was a sociable one. Dinner parties were frequent and festive. My mother served seven-course meals; my father lined up empty wine bottles at his feet. The dining room was tiny but the walnut table was huge; you couldn't get into a chair on the far side unless people stood up to let you past. Crossing your legs during the meal was impossible; pushed back even a foot, chairs scraped against the wall. Six, sometimes eight adults ate and drank in that room until midnight, with children watching from the doorway or playing in the basement. Crystal goblets were made to sing. Spoons were made to dangle off noses. Holiday feasts, served in mid-afternoon, often climaxed with dads beached on the living-room floor, eyes closed, hands folded across chests. Mischievous sons sometimes jumped onto Dromedarian bellies. Bursts of snoring snapped the air.

The Forans also hosted dance parties. The twenty-fourth of May provided one occasion for a gathering, until home fireworks displays were banned. My parents held winter parties with costumes and themes, and eight-tracks of Tom Jones and Englebert Humperdinck blasting from the stereo. In summers our aboveground swimming pool would be jammed with adults making whirlpools to the accompaniment of Hank Williams or Ginette Reno from a cassette player on the deck. For a child these were wondrous events, vivid and mysterious: a glimpse at the ways of the grown-up world. I knew the faces of most guests in our house, and recognized them to be neighbours on the block, colleagues from my father's office, old friends from up north. I knew these faces well enough to wonder about who wasn't present, who wasn't part of the group. None of the Willowtree Estate people were colleagues or friends — that I accepted. But a question stuck in my mind. Surely they belonged to the first category? Surely, given the proximity — our house was closer to the outer row of Willowtree units than to the families up the road — we were all neighbours?

CHAPTER IV

Newry, the first town Mary and I came upon inside the border, lay along the bottom of a river valley. An ashen sky mirrored the hues of housing estates and shops, buildings and churches, a canal choked in slime. Once a marketing town, Newry now traded in nationalist paramilitaries and security forces; once a proud Catholic community, it now staggered under fifty per cent unemployment, exoduses to Belfast and Dundalk, the twin yoke of overt army and RUC enforcement of one set of laws, and covert IRA marshalling of the ghettos based on other rules. They flew the Irish tricolour in certain Newry estates. They made bombs in certain Newry sitting rooms. Ulstermen declared the town "not our side" and gave it a wide berth; security forces patrolled the streets with wary aggression, forced bluster. Soldiers were still sniped at, still mortar-bombed, still killed. Even nationalists had trouble mustering a good word; outstanding footballers in Newry, Sean McNally had always assured me.

A decade ago, when Sean and I passed through the town on weekends, it was ringed in concertina wire and checkpoints to slow the pace of insurrection. Now, fitted out for the nineties, Newry was monitored using mounted cameras and corkscrewing helicopters, towers with radar eyes. Foot patrols continued to intimidate the natives, however, and traffic slowed as we neared the town centre, permitting us a close-up of a six-man squad — double the normal Belfast size — pointing their weapons at shoppers. The square had a Bank of Ireland, a boarded-up Salvation Army hospice and a Saint Colman's Hall with bearded gargoyles gazing down in vacant displeasure at the street. Our itinerary had included a pit-stop in Newry, for tea and a diaper change. But I saw no pub, saw too many guns and decided our daughter could wait. We drove on.

North County Down was luxuriant as always, the Mourne Mountains declining, the Lagan winding its way to Belfast. A rolling landscape of farmhouses and barns, dogs in fields and tractors puttering along the motorway shoulder, the countryside banished thoughts of civil strife. Army towers were still visible, but were either behind us, back towards the border, or else ahead, covering southern approaches to the capital. In between was a Troubles-free zone, an Ulster theme park memorialized in song — "My Lagan Love" and "Star of the County Down".

The second checkpoint, hidden over a rise to discourage hasty U-turns, had me gearing down in a panic. A dozen soldiers stood on the tarmac, with more positioned in the brush. Two jeeps parked on the shoulder. The queue was twenty cars long, and at a standstill.

"Shit," I said.

"Relax," said Mary.

While relaxing, I recalled other roadblock encounters. Being stopped with a McNally had never been a problem. Questions were answered in a calm, civil manner; no information was divulged beyond the legal requirements — name and address, where we were coming from and going to — and no family member, including Maureen, ever cracked a smile at the interrogator. The family had experienced plenty of checkpoints, and, for a period, under the worst circumstances. They knew not to provoke. They had discipline. Only afterwards would Patricia mutter a word of dismay and Sean an epithet. Once, Sean commented on the effect of having a soldier with a British accent aim a gun at his head a few metres, or a few kilometres, from his home. His skin crawled, he confessed. Taunting words pressed his lips.

I was never stopped in a vehicle with Mairtin.

Years before, Mary and I had travelled with friends to a music festival in Donegal. From Dublin the quickest route was through Fermanagh, meaning an hour inside the North. As always, the artificiality of the border startled; a bumpy country road that bifurcated fields in the Irish Republic was abruptly a bumpy country road inside a region of the United Kingdom, with the fields themselves sometimes half in, half out. The crossing looked undefended, but we ran into a roadblock a kilometre beyond. South Fermanagh was staunch nationalist country. No surprise, the operation was fearsome: a small armoured booth beside the road, a tower set back to read license plates and photograph faces, speed bumps. The car we were in, a Morris Minor, had imperfect wipers. The rain fell hard.

John Bagley rolled down the driver's window. John was a friend from UCD who now taught high school in County Clare. A gentle, soft-spoken man, he was one of those Dubliners who seemed more interested in Chinese history and jazz music than in Northern Ireland. Other friends did have strident views and republican politics. But not John.

"Could I see a driver's licence, please?"

The soldier had dark eyebrows and clear skin. He looked thirty. (British troops stationed in the North tended to be pimply teenagers.) His accent, though, was pronounced: working-class, possibly east end London.

John feigned frisking his pockets. "I don't have it on me," he answered in a cold voice.

"Have you other identification, sir?"

"No."

"The law requires you to carry identification in a vehicle," the soldier said.

"What law?"

Understanding John's question, the man changed his tone. "The law of the United Kingdom," he answered.

"We're only driving up to Donegal."

"You're inside Northern Ireland."

"I'm on an Irish road."

"You're subject to British laws."

Rain on the roof half-drowned the conversation. The windows had fogged over. From the back seat, the scene was surreal and the silence crackled with tension. We were in the middle of nowhere; we were refusing to co-operate; there were no witnesses. I had seen photos and TV footage of similar scenarios. The car pockmarked with bullets, overturned in a ditch, bodies slumped against the splintered glass or spilling out the doors; a uniformed spin doctor with a proper accent explaining that the driver had tried to flee, that the victims had been known to authorities, that he couldn't say any more at this moment, for security reasons.

I decided to intervene. Grabbing Mary's passport, I waved two foreign documents in the soldier's face.

"I'm talking to this gentleman," he said, not taking his eyes off John.

"We're from —"

"I'm talking to this gentleman."

I withdrew the passports.

John, who had so far refused to meet the soldier's gaze, now turned to him. "Say what you like," he answered, "as far as I'm concerned, I'm still in Ireland."

Water poured off the man's helmet. Still glaring at John, he made a gesture with his weapon. Two more soldiers hustled up to the car and raised their rifles to our heads.

"Have any of *you* identification?" he asked us.

We nearly threw our documents at him. The soldier refused to reach inside, and John refused to forward the papers. I acted as relay. He studied the birth certificate of the front-seat passenger, a graduate student from Waterford named Ed Walshe, and our passports.

"Rains in this country, doesn't it?" he said to Mary and me.

Our agreement was unequivocal.

"Identification is required by all drivers in the United Kingdom," he told John.

John still looked ahead.

"John! . . ." said Ed.

"Understood," muttered John.

The soldier paused, as if deciding, then returned the documents. The thump, thump on the roof could have passed for distant gunfire.

"Hope the weather is better in Donegal."

"Can we leave?" asked John.

The man nodded.

Silence reigned until we crossed back into the Republic. John's hands shook when he lifted them from the wheel. Ed Walshe stared out the window.

"Bernadette-fucking-Devlin, are we?" he finally said.

John apologized. "Must have been his accent," he explained in his old voice.

"You didn't like it?"

"I didn't like hearing it in County Fermanagh. From a man telling me what to do, where to go, because he had a weapon and I didn't. Bad enough all the local edjits with guns. Now a foreigner?"

Recalling the incident, and anticipating my possible encounter with a British soldier, I took comfort in a key difference: the man's accent had sounded a particular bell in John Bagley. You had to be Irish to hear it. You probably had to be Irish Catholic.

Our queue was down to five cars. All the vehicles were being waved through by a tall soldier with a walkie-talkie strapped to his chest and a finger on the trigger of a rifle. Judging by the speed of his decisions and his inattentiveness to drivers, licences were what counted.

"They're letting everyone through," I said to Mary.

The car ahead of us was waved on. I pulled up. The soldier glanced down at the plate, up at my face. He made a motion. Over to the curve, it ordered. Immediately.

"Shit," I repeated.

"Must be your beard."

"Moo-cow!" said Anna, noticing the fields beyond the checkpoint.

Relax, we both silently agreed.

"What's the crack, Chuck?" asked Sean.

"Cold," I answered.

"Didn't you wait inside the flat?"

"It's warmer out here."

"No fire?"

"I was by myself."

"I know what you mean," he agreed.

It was the morning of December 24, 1983, and Sean and I were driving up to Belfast. Christmas had been grimly augured. An IRA car bomb had exploded outside Harrods department store in London the week before. Six people had been killed, ninety-one injured. Outraged Londoners had shown stiff upper lips on television; Margaret Thatcher had flown over to the North for a brief visit, including a stop at an army headquarters in County Armagh notorious for the shoot-to-kill policies of its staff. While waiting for Sean in a freezing apartment — my flatmates had already left for the holidays — I had glanced at a newspaper report in which the IRA disavowed the bomb as "unapproved". The organization regretted these particular deaths, but not the deaths of civilians in England; in war, everyone was a target.

But I wasn't paying much attention to the news. Only three months before, I would have been pleased with myself for being able to read Irish newspapers without a historical dictionary. Already, though, recognizing references to James Connolly, tossing off allusions to the Fenians, exchanging banter using the acronyms for different paramilitary groups, turning grim during discussions of Paisley's secret army and Gerry Adams' murky past; these skills were feeling more mimicked than learned, a vocabulary of surface rather than substance. Much of the bluster seemed rhetorical. Much of it sounded like pub chat.

The drive was cold, too. Icy rain kept turning to snow. When we reached the house at four o'clock, night was fast approaching. Our arrival coincided with Maureen's return in the Granada. We embraced on the front steps, snowflakes swarming us like insects. Her hands were ice.

"Not a nice day," I said, once inside the hallway.

"Awful."

"Perfect for sitting by a fire."

"With a pot of tea," she concurred.

"How did you do, Ma?" asked Sean, wiping snow from his hair.

"I haven't played so poorly in ages," she replied. "My thoughts were elsewhere, I suppose."

"Played what?"

"Golf."

"Pardon?"

"Only nine holes, Chuck, I mean Cathal. Wouldn't have missed welcoming you and Sean. Had to be back for that."

"But it's snowing."

"The wind was high as well," she sighed. "Nearly carried one of my shots off into the lough."

"I'm impressed."

"I'm frozen."

"I'll put the kettle on," said Sean.

Maureen was a woman of expressive sighs and unexpressed sorrows. She had a soft voice and a unique intonation. Her sentences often began high, dropped in the middle, then climbed back up towards their endings. Key phrases tended to trail off. Their retreat obliged the listener either to ask her to repeat herself, or else to stand closer, devote absolute attention. The intimacy pleased her. She could be voluble in one-to-one chats but tended to stay quiet during the more freewheeling sitting-room sessions. While talking, Maureen liked to rest her hand on the other person's forearm. When frustrated, she struck out with both hands; when sad, she etched circles and lines in the air.

Mairtin had her eyes and Bernie her laugh. Ciaran showed identical crow's-feet when he smiled. Sean's gentleness was clearly learned at home. Patricia's breathless whisper was her mother's, a half-octave higher.

Maureen McNally had raised five children. She had kept several houses. Once she had worked in a shop to help out; now she was employed at the local church, more for pleasure than for pay. Born in the Falls Road, she had lived her entire life in West and North Belfast.

Travels abroad had focused on visiting emigrant siblings in Canada, England and the States. Holidays had been taken mostly in Antrim and Down before 1969, in Dublin and Kerry since. Belfast was her home. The house on Leeson Avenue was her nest. It was also a city she had ceased wanting to live in fourteen years before. It remained a house she would gladly have sold.

By evening, it was also a full house: five occupied bedrooms, all but one with two sleepers. I shared a large front bedroom with Sean. Patricia, still queasy from the Stranraer–Larne ferry ride that morning, had brought along a fellow nurse — Kate, from Australia. They took a smaller room. With the parents in the other main bedroom, that left Mairtin, home since early in the month, sharing with Ciaran, and Bernie in the chamber on the lower landing. Quixote had his kitchen basket. Aengus had the rug before the fire.

The dog sported a red ribbon around his neck, with a bow at the front. While I tried patting him on the skull in greeting, he tried devouring the bow, swiveling his snout around in frustration. His growls were playful, even festive; I slipped my hands back in my pockets.

Everyone assembled for a Christmas Eve Ulster fry, McNally-style: bacon and sausage, fried and scrambled eggs, boiled potatoes and potato bread, broiled tomatoes, brown bread and grilled pancakes, toast. For dessert, there was apple tart with cream, creamed coffees and white teas, a plate of biscuits and sweets. Table decorum was, as always, civil, and conversation was civil-tongued in a funny, gently barbed Belfast way. Lots of catching up was done: child with parent, sibling with sibling. All were congratulated for successes, commiserated with over problems. Interest in each others' affairs ran high, and was sincere. But the stuffing was also taken out of Mairtin; Patricia and Bernie were both given a bit of the stick. James and Maureen mostly watched, quiet, pleased. James refilled glasses. Maureen poured hot drops.

Guests weren't forgotten. Happily, though, for the first time I was just Chuck/Cathal; no longer a blow-in; adjunct family now. The focus fell on Kate. She was a tall woman with a lanky torso and a fresh face: tawny freckled skin and sea-green eyes, a continent-sized smile. Not shy, she spoke brightly in an accent that drowned most words in a vocable soup of *yeehhs* and *eehhs* and *ggiitts*. Her love of, and pride in, Australian vernacular didn't help, and with secret pleasure my eyes flitted from McNally to McNally as they puzzled over Kate's drawn-out vowels and chipper idioms. As host, James suffered the most. Once his gaze settled on a guest, the questions poured out: about Australia in general and Perth in particular, about her parents and siblings, her calico cat and myna bird.

But his poker-face kept cracking. First he made feeble attempts to elicit repetitions by tugging on his ear and apologizing for creeping deafness. (His hearing was perfect.) He also kept drawing closer to the young woman, nodding in enthusiasm and begging more details. The furrow across his forehead, the panicked sucking on his cigarette: you could almost read his thoughts: *Mother of God, what is this girl saying?*

Tonight was Kate's initiation. Tonight the McNallys would be on their best behaviour with her. Maybe one or two jokes, a wee jab — to judge humour levels, irony marks. If Kate seemed willing, even able, to spar, to crack, tomorrow would be looser, much sillier.

We fought to do the washing-up. Maureen refused to leave the kitchen, but kept to one side while Mairtin and I bent over the sink. He had been his usual quiet self during the meal, but did show some impatience when ribbed about life in London, a city he was clearly not predisposed to like. The English capital was, in turn, equally predisposed not to like people like him: another Mick, another Paddy. He was there finishing his graduate degree, nothing else.

"What was the reaction to the Harrods bombing?" I asked.

"I left before it happened."

I nodded.

"But I suspect they're a bit upset," he added flatly.

"A bit, Mairtin?" said his mother.

"I don't think I can really say how the English might react," he continued. "I don't know many Londoners. It's a whole other country over there, you know. Certainly their opinions on the situation are of no interest. Even if I were to meet an Englishman who was sympathetic to the republican position, I wouldn't pay him much heed. He still wouldn't know what the crack was."

"The crack?"

"What's actually going on here. Why nationalists are motivated to do what they do. Who's to blame, ultimately. What's to be done."

"Do you defend the IRA to the English?"

My own question took me by surprise. So did my voice: I sounded angry, impatient. But Mairtin, still rinsing pots, simply smiled.

"I don't discuss politics any more, Chuck. For sure not in London." Maureen sighed.

"Is bombing a department store 'politics'?"

Mairtin straightened. He turned to me, his face stern but still gentle. I braced myself for a lecture.

"They're wee boys doing most of these terrible things," he began softly. "Boys sent out by older men to look after the worst business. I was a boy too, ten years ago. I know how it feels."

The pause was lengthy. Maureen sighed again and left the kitchen. Mairtin watched her go.

"Say you're from a neighbourhood in West Belfast," he resumed. "A street full of families you've known your entire life. Your mates live nearby, go to the same school, belong to the same club. Terrible injustices are being done to these people. Done by soldiers from another country with strange accents who patrol the streets like they own them and treat ordinary citizens like criminals. Done by a sectarian police force in collusion with the army, in collusion with a state committed to keeping you and your kind in your place. Suppose you're eighteen or nineteen, strong and full of fight, and you're watching all this happen. What are you going to do?"

"I suppose you'll —"

Mairtin crossed the kitchen. He checked the small dining room, then closed the door. His voice dropped even lower. "Suppose your own family has been made to suffer. Suppose businesses have been burned and bombed. Suppose you've watched the dreams of your own parents — the dreams they had for themselves, for their children — be destroyed. What's a young lad going to do? A lad living in a particular place, you know, at a particular time. How would *you* have reacted if you'd been born here, or if the same things had happened in Canada?"

What about me? The question stood.

I hesitated.

"How would Chuck have reacted to what, Mairtin?" asked James, entering suddenly.

"Nothing, Da."

"I'm interested."

Mairtin repeated the conversation to his father.

"That's hardly a fair question."

"Why not?"

"Because he wasn't born here. Because things aren't that way in Canada. Because —"

"I don't mind answering," I interrupted.

"We don't interrogate our guests," said James, glancing at his son. "Not in this house."

"Chuck's plenty old enough to decide whether he wants to answer."

"I realize that. I was only —"

"I raised the subject, James," I said.

"You did?"

There was a silence.

"Go on, then," said the elder McNally, crossing his arms.

I made the mistake of looking at him, not Mairtin. I chose my words to please a father I admired, not to speak the truth about what his son had experienced.

"Violence is violence," I summarized, the words ringing hollow in my ears. "It can't ever be justified — not by age, circumstance, anything."

"Aye," said James, clearly relieved.

"I guess things *are* different in Canada," said Mairtin, clearly disgusted.

Maureen reappeared. She sized up the situation. "They're clamouring for tea in the sitting room," she said. "Put the kettle on, will you, James? And you two — leave the rest of the washing-up until later."

We obliged.

"What about the news?" asked James.

"Let's have a night off from the news," answered his wife. "It won't do us much harm, I'm sure."

James seemed doubtful. Still, he promised to remain in the kitchen until the tea was made. I opened the sitting-room door onto a blast of heat. Seated on the couch and chairs were Patricia and Kate, Bernie and Ciaran, Sean. Sprawled before the fire was Aengus. To one side of the dog stood Quixote, cleaning himself. The cat looked slick.

"Aengus gave Quixote a good lathering," offered Ciaran. "You just missed it."

The empty chair belonged to James. Numb with shame about the argument, I sank down on the carpet near the animals. A smell curled my nostrils. The odour wasn't coal or conifer tree or even dog saliva. On TV, a bearded man was conducting an orchestra through a Christmas medley. The music was for elevators. The man, dressed in a tuxedo left open at his wide-winged shirt collar, had a unique conducting style — cadaver-stiff, his face devoid of expression. Only his baton arm moved, from the elbow down, the motion as regular as a metronome bar.

"Who's that?"

"James Last," answered Patricia. "Mother and Father are mad for his music."

"He looks ill."

"He's from Derry," said Ciaran.

"Germany," corrected Sean.

"I thought he was from Derry?"

"You're thinking of Phil Coulter," said Bernie.

"Who?" asked Kate.

"He still looks ill," I said.

"The music's a bit dull, right enough," said Patricia. "Only don't tell the parents. They'd be crushed."

The parents arrived with trays. One held tea and fruitcake, the other mugs and plates.

"Lovely," said Patricia.

"More tea?" wondered Kate.

The Australian rose and, enquiring about the washroom, excused herself. She closed the door. It clicked back open. She tried again. The door stayed shut for three seconds. An embarrassed, exasperated laugh from the hallway got me to my feet. "It's okay," I whispered to her through the crack. I shouldered it closed.

"Isn't James Last brilliant?" asked Maureen.

"Mmm," said several of her children.

"He's from Derry, isn't he?"

"Who?" asked James.

"The fella on the screen."

"I believe he's Dutch," said her husband.

"Phil Coulter's German," I threw in, sitting back down on the floor.

"Is he?" asked Maureen.

"He must be famous in Canada?" asked James.

"Who?"

"Phil Coulter."

"Never heard of him," I admitted.

"Ah," said James, lighting a cigarette.

"James Last is from Toronto, isn't he, Chuck?" asked Sean.

"Stop!" said Maureen.

The smell was overpowering. I had to ask about it.

"Aengus is cooking," explained Ciaran.

"Sorry?"

"Touch the dog."

Aengus lay inches from the hearth. His exposed eye blinked. His tongue dangled from his mouth. Reaching out to rub his belly, I pulled back instantly at the burn. His skull was equally searing. Examining him more closely, I noticed the tongue was dry as sandpaper, the eye filmy. Only the dilation of his nostrils confirmed that the dog was still breathing.

"So the smell . . . ?"

"Dog fur," answered Sean.

"Why doesn't he move?"

"We aren't sure," said Maureen. "We think he falls into a trance, just staring at the flames, his body temperature climbing. Sounds lovely, doesn't it?"

"Ciaran had to drag Aengus away from the fire the other night," offered James. "We were worried he might explode."

Kate returned.

"There's a funny smell," she commented.

"James Last is from Perth, isn't he?" Sean asked her.

"The sick fella on the telly?" she answered.

"Close the door, will you, Kate dear," said James.

Later, long after midnight, with the fire stoked for morning and a half-baked Aengus let out the back, I helped load the dishwasher. Kitchen conversations with Maureen were my secret passion. I loved the McNally kitchen. Cupboard shelves overflowed with soup cans and marmalade jars, packets of biscuits and tins of tea; the counter was crowded with a breadbox, fruit bowls, mug trees. The double-door refrigerator burst with supplies and the pantry in the washing room was overstocked. Even the smells were abundant: fat drippings at the bottom of the broiler, the sugar tang of opened biscuit tins, the fug of grounds stewing in an unemptied pot.

The room itself was spacious and private, with smoked-glass doors to seal it from the rest of the house and stools for sitting. At the rear was a chamber that led to the garden. At either end were apertures: a door onto the coal shed, a window into the greenhouse. People ate breakfast in the kitchen, downed quick cups of tea, listened to the news. They also gathered to chat. As a meeting place, it was less formal than the sitting room: one talked while cooking soup, folding clothes, boiling water. Conversations were presumed open, for any and all to hear.

"I'm so happy for you," Maureen said.

"Why?"

"You never had to ask yourself the sorts of questions Mairtin put to you earlier. Never had to make those decisions, live with those errors. Childhood isn't supposed to involve such trauma and terror. Here, in this awful place, children grow up too quick."

"Too hard?"

"Usually that, too."

"Sometimes I wonder if maybe I would have benefited from having to ask those questions when I —"

Maureen interrupted me, a rare occurrence. "There's no good in it," she said. "Believe you me. The experience isn't worth the cost. Ask Mairtin."

She paused. I busied myself with the dishes.

"Not just him, though," she resumed. "What about Sean, with being shot at in pubs, having friends arrested and killed. And Patricia, with all she's witnessed at the hospital. Or wee Bernie, after the bomb at the Poly . . . ."

"You're right," I amended. "I wasn't thinking."

She rested her hand on my arm. "The boys got out at least, thank God. Boys are more worry than girls. So quick to anger, so full of violence. You can't trust them to control themselves. . . . Of course, men are worse than women, too."

"Thrawn?"

"Nice word," she agreed.

"But you're not still worried?—"

"Sean's gone, for sure. He's too gentle a soul for here. And Mairtin has little choice in the matter. With his history, he's almost no chance of a career in the North. Just Ciaran left to fret about now."

"He's like his father," I offered.

"Bright, handsome, popular," summarized Maureen. "A big man around town already. As was James . . . ." She was silent again. "But I want Ciaran out as well. Out of Belfast and out of the North. And Bernie, and even sweet Patricia. Only then will I stop worrying about my children."

Maureen McNally's hair had been white since I first met her. Her face was lined around the mouth and eyes; her irises were often shot through with red. What I had always suspected about this lovely woman — that she had been living in a permanent state of anxiety since 1969 — was confirmed.

"Sleep well," said Maureen.

I promised to try.

James McNally used the government compensation for the Mountainview to make two purchases. First, he and Maureen bought a new house. Though their apartment in South Belfast had been outside the unofficial boundaries of the Troubles, they had no hesitation about looking back inside the zone. The conflict was, after all, far from permanent; in six months or a year it would likely be over. Fortwilliam Park wasn't an option, but the Antrim Road in the blocks around the top of the street was. Houses were large and, as ever in Belfast, modestly priced. And houses along that section of the road were now owned by both Catholics and Protestants. Farther below, Antrim Road dwellers were nationalists; farther up, they were unionists. In 1971, the family moved back into their old neighbourhood.

James also bought another pub. Here he did show caution, signs of being chastened. Since 1969, pubs had continued to be burned or bombed around Belfast, often while full of customers. Those not bombed ended up closing out of fear or frustration. Worried that his reputation would attract another mob, James bought a business in Antrim, a Protestant town forty kilometres beyond Divis Hill. In Antrim, he hoped, he would be anonymous: simply a publican, albeit a Catholic, albeit a Belfast man, seeking to earn a living away from the madness that gripped the capital.

He would also be a publican attempting to practise his profession. Among the earliest social casualties of the Troubles was Belfast pub culture. Locals were being bombed, or just shutting down, at an alarming rate around the north and west parts of the city. Those still open had to deal with a nervous, dwindling clientele. Why risk death for a pint? Emerging from the ashes were drinking clubs. These were wartime businesses: paramilitary-owned and positioned in the hearts of ghettos, safe from planted bombs and bullet sprays. The movement was from public houses to private clubs; from attractive, often elegant surroundings to elevated bunkers; from open doors to galvanized wire-mesh gates and security cameras with swivelling eyes; from professional barmen to retired volunteers; from expertly pulled pints to flat beer, warm soda; from soft music (or, better, no music at all) to blaring republican or loyalist ballads. The movement was from an environment with the prospect of friendly chats with strangers to an environment of the same old carry-on with the same old crowd; from the remote possibility of encountering an opinion or perspective that might challenge your own to the repetition of rote ideology among the like-minded. The movement was from a tradition of sociability, strained but not broken by sectarianism, to one of anti-sociability, demarcated by tribe, delineated by place.

Things were different now, of course. James and Maureen were well aware of the new situation. They knew their streets were being patrolled by British soldiers there to police a prolonged civil disturbance. They even recognized that North Belfast was proving unusually strife-ridden, unusually vulnerable. But the McNally parents had been born in the wake of the pogroms of the early 1920s. They had witnessed and survived the blitz. Equally, they had experienced the easing of tensions in the fifties and sixties, the expansion of the middle class, even the glimmer of hope lit by the civil rights marches and demonstrations. For them, August 1969 had ushered in a phase quickly dubbed "the current Troubles", in honour of earlier dark times. The current Troubles were bad, all right, but they too would eventually end. Then people would be able to speak of the 1969–71 or 1969–72 Troubles, and compare them to earlier incarnations, and express grim satisfaction at surviving still more bad Belfast history.

Mairtin was a teenager when the Mountainview burned down, Ciaran a boy. All the McNally children were in school the spring before the riots; all returned once classes resumed in September. For the youngest kids, confined to the neighbourhood, tanks and troops in lower North Belfast went unobserved. What Bernie and Ciaran witnessed was the abrupt rise in tension as they passed by Protestant schools, where kids like them exchanged taunts with kids not like them, and where gangs sometimes chased boys up the road and into nearby Alexandra Park and gave out hidings, terrible scares. Mornings were for hasty insults; after-class was for leisurely fistfights and periodic running battles. Their mother made them wear coats over their school uniforms, regardless of the weather.

For Patricia, the school year at the Dominican convent towards the top of Fortwilliam Park, where she was about to start Grade 9, began with a special assembly. The nuns asked that all girls whose families had suffered during the riots step forward. Patricia remained in place, but others identified themselves. They were given clothes and money, their tuition fees lowered or even dropped. Girls faced routine harassment from soldiers at the gates, leading to sharp words between nuns in habits and recruits in combat gear. In 1970–71, Patricia's school averaged ten bomb scares a day. Each call obliged staff to hustle the entire student body into the courtyard while teachers searched in toilets and under desks for incendiary devices. Classes went on despite the crack of gunfire or the shattering of glass. Once, while Patricia was writing a final exam, a bomb detonated nearby blew in the classroom windows. Students were made to wait in the corridor for an hour. Ushered back, they found the windows boarded and the exam set to continue; the proctors promised to take the explosion into consideration when marking the papers. Off campus, Patricia also had to make certain her school crest was kept hidden.

In 1970, Sean graduated from primary to secondary school on the campus of St. Mary's in Barrack Street. On the first day of class, soldiers stormed the building in search of stone-throwers. St. Mary's was located off the bottom of Divis Street in West Belfast. This made it adjacent to both the Divis Flats—a notorious battleground for clashes between ghetto Catholics and security forces—and the Lower Falls Road, principal recruiting area for the IRA. The Divis Flats themselves were hardcore. Built only a few years before, the huge six-storey complexes of narrow dwellings housed many Catholic families who had been burned out of surrounding streets. A breeding-ground for paramilitaries, as well as home to a lot of unemployed, much-put-upon people, the flats spelled big trouble for the police and army, who frequently surrounded the complex and occasionally carried out raids on apartments amid clanging bin-lids, varieties of missiles and sniper fire from nearby houses or the Divis Tower.

Sean went rioting in the flats during lunch-hour. On their way up Divis Street he and his friends would remove their school crests, attached to jacket breasts by a pin, and cut in behind St. Peter's pro-Cathedral. The Brits were there every day; all it took was a few stones to start a rumble. Piles of rocks and bottles awaited them for that purpose. (During more serious confrontations, weapons included steel darts, nail grenades and flaming "petrol bombs".) Fly-in rioters were welcomed by the locals. Heaving bottles and bricks, the St. Mary's rioters advanced when the soldiers withdrew, then pulled back into stairwells and flats when the Brits surged ahead. The action had its limits. If the army started lifting people, everyone disappeared. Likewise if tear gas was used or someone got hit by a rubber bullet.

Mairtin was enrolled at St. Malachy's on the lower Antrim Road. The school, which his father had attended, was among the most respected of private Catholic institutions in Belfast. It was known for the quality of its education and the severity of its discipline. Priests were stern patriarchs; lay headmasters brooked no dissent, showed no leniency. Unofficial school policy demanded that students check the Troubles at the front gate. Given the location of the campus — a few hundred metres from the Crumlin Jail and courthouse, a block up from the Orange Hall at Carlisle Circus — this required extreme order and much wilful blinkering. State scholarships swelled the ranks at St. Malachy's with boys from nearby Cliftonville and New Lodge, the Bone and Ardoyne. Unlike Mairtin, these kids weren't returning from class to comfortable houses in prosperous neighbourhoods. They were returning to decrepit terraces with dads on the broo, brothers interned or convicted, army raids at midnight. School officials might insist that students concentrate on their math and science, their history and Latin, but they had no control over the exchange of information, the circulation of stories and rumours.

For Mairtin McNally, already obliged to cover the St. Malachy crest while walking down the Antrim Road — a classmate of Sean's had been killed by a sniper because of his school jacket — and already enraged by the destruction of his father's pub, the school policy was ostrich-like. Conflict was everywhere in North and West Belfast. Trouble waited outside the guarded school gate; sometimes, it ventured into the compound.

Back in the Antrim Road house, the McNally parents struggled to maintain some semblance of an ordinary life. It was indeed a terrible time. Northern Ireland was shaken by a bomb blast per day in 1970. The first British soldier to die in the North since Partition was killed near Duncairn Gardens in February of 1971. In March the previously defence-minded IRA took to the offensive. Three teenage Scots, members of the Royal Highland Fusiliers, were chatted up by locals in a city pub; later that night their bodies were discovered in a North Belfast ditch. The introduction of internment in August sent the city into a frenzy. Some three hundred and forty-two men, most of them unconnected with any political organization, every single one of them Catholic, were imprisoned without charge. The riots that followed were prolonged. On a single day, twelve people in Belfast were killed, including a priest administering last rites. Hundreds more were burned from their homes. The IRA lost its first recruit during a battle in the Falls Road. Rumours of torture during interrogations of internees leaked out. The riots intensified, and the snipings, bombings and murders took on the sheen of a guerrilla-style engagement. Protestant fears surged. Loyalist paranoia turned bloody. The RUC hired more recruits. The British called in more troops.

On January 30, 1972, thirteen protesters were killed by British paratroopers during a civil rights demonstration in Derry. The marchers were unarmed, and some were shot in the back while fleeing for cover.

Maureen and James encouraged their children to continue to play football in the Ardoyne, to go to the club with friends, to take gymnastic lessons. The family attended mass together at Holy Family Church. On Sunday afternoons they drove up the Falls Road to visit Maureen's elderly father, who had witnessed rioting out front of his house, and down into South Belfast, where James's mother lived. But the parents also insisted on escorting their children most places, even just around the neighbourhood. James, an avid radio listener, would duly announce changes to the Belfast map — where there had been trouble, which streets to avoid now. Maureen, constantly worried, constantly anxious, would demand that Mairtin ring from the Polytechnic, that Sean not cut through the Waterworks on his way home from the club, that they all walk facing oncoming traffic.

Maureen also began going through Mairtin's pockets. Her eldest son had turned hard and strange. He kept odd hours. He had new friends. He refused to explain where he was going, where he had been. He took calls from unfamiliar voices, informed them he would ring back and then left the house. He also lectured his parents on the war. That was what it was. That was the situation. The British were colluding with the Orange state. It was us against them. It was us *or* them.

There were terrible arguments.

Ironically, Maureen felt most at ease when her eldest boys were up in Antrim town with their father. Mairtin and Sean helped out in the pub on weekends. James had renamed the bar "The Circle", in honour of the floor arrangement of his previous business, despite the fact that the new room featured a traditional long counter. No matter; this was a business, not his parents' pub, not a place for friends or community, not even an operation he foresaw handing on to his sons. Antrim people liked the bar, though, liked its new owner and its new owner's wife and children. The business thrived. James, happy to be back doing what he loved, made improvements. The risk of being blown up seemed slight. The Troubles hadn't spread much to Protestant Antrim; the Troubles hadn't, in fact, spread much outside Belfast and Derry, parts of South Armagh. He renovated, hired more staff, paid musicians. He opened a restaurant upstairs; Maureen did some of the cooking.

In Antrim, the older McNally sons were simply boys working in a pub. Belfast boys, admittedly, but that city was a long hour's drive away. On weekends Mairtin and Sean brought up schoolwork and slept on mats behind the counter. Country air was good for sleeping. Small-town life was good crack. The brothers felt relaxed in Antrim town; they joked and kidded more. The parents felt the same.

But Belfast had to be returned to: schools and churches, clubs and friends, the house on Antrim Road. Once back on their feet, what James and Maureen could provide for their children was a home outside the enclaves. They could provide a stable, supportive environment: unconditional love, unconditional acceptance. What neither parent could do, however, was prevent Mairtin from turning nineteen in 1972, or Patricia from reaching seventeen, or Sean from celebrating his fifteenth birthday; what they could not do was keep young people from feeling the turmoil young people feel, with their simultaneous needs to translate impulse into action, however rash or shallow; what neither James nor Maureen could do was send these teenagers to their rooms, draw the drapes and lock the door, in the hope that Belfast would miraculously calm or that near-adults would miraculously revert to being children again.

The McNally children had little recourse to memories of another Belfast. They had grown up in what looked like a military state in the throes of an irregular war. For youngsters there was no validity in speaking of the "current Troubles" or the "present situation". All they saw were the Troubles, the situation. Declaring the mess certain to end soon became meaningless to the school-aged generation; as time passed, they forgot all about pre-1969. A city of tank patrols and military road-blocks, of street battles and apartment-tower snipers, of bombed-out buildings and blood-smeared sidewalks, became the only city they knew, and, more important, could *envision* ever knowing, through either recollection or conjecture.

That state of mind became a concrete reality for James and Maureen McNally one night in November 1972. The call came late in the evening. At the other end of the line was an RUC officer. Their son Mairtin was being held in Castlereagh, over in East Belfast. The charges? Resisting arrest. Suspected criminal activity. Membership in the IRA.

I awoke early on Christmas morning. At eight o'clock, with mass barely an hour away, I decided it was safe to brew tea. Nine mugs were arranged on the tray. Nine drops of milk were poured. I found the largest, most industrial teapot in the McNally collection, a stainless-steel urn that dated back to the Antrim pub, and brimmed it with bobbing tea bags. Again I did reconnaissance — opening doors, checking for the dog, making certain the stairwell was clear. Remarkably, I reached the top of the landing without spillage. Two mugs were assigned to all bedrooms except the one next to the bathroom. I studied my watch: forty-five minutes to mass. I rapped, not too hard, not too soft, on each door. Perfect knocks they were, too.

Silence.

A car passed on the street. Wind penetrated the bathroom window, tried picking the lock. Aengus scratched himself in the hallway below.

Finally, someone stirred. The commotion came from the room nearest the top of the stairs, where I sat. The knob turned. The door pulled open. A bare foot crossed the threshold to where both mugs stood in plain sight. The foot made contact with one mug, barely missed the other. A voice commented "Ouch," and then "Shit!" The accent was not local.

Kate, in a nightgown, gazed down at the liquid darkening the carpet. She retied a strand of hair behind her ears and looked over at the stairs. Her eyes were cloudy with sleep.

"Not your fault," I said, smiling weakly.

"What is it?"

"A cup of tea."

"What's it doing there?"

"I'll get a cloth," I answered.

I mopped up the tea and withdrew the other mugs. Kate declared the custom "daffy" and went back to sleep. When Patricia, my church partner, turned up in the kitchen at four minutes to nine, she glanced at the sink of tea cups. "I thought you and Mother loaded the dishwasher last night," she commented.

I made an excuse.

Sean joined us at the front door. "The Hulk awaits," he said, turning up his jacket collar.

The neighbourhood still slumbered. Curtains were drawn, chimneys were smokeless. Only two black dogs were out, escorting groggy owners around the block. We trotted with bowed heads. At the curb across from the church, I raised my sights to admire Cave Hill. The road dissolved into its wooded west slope, and the earth higher up was laced with fog trails. The crown had disappeared in cloud.

The Church of the Resurrection was aptly named. Twice it had been blown up; twice it had been repaired and reopened. The building resembled a hockey rink — squat and low, with a sloping front, walls of red brick and a roof of black shingles. The main entrance featured a rolling door, as on a garage, and another steel and glass door behind it. The steps were protected by an iron fence. Nothing in the design was especially warm or welcoming. The church looked best closed; it photographed most dramatically in a downpour.

Church elders had taken note of the austerity, Sean explained at the curb. To compensate, they had commissioned statues from a Cork artist with a reputation for expressive work. The church had ordered a Mother of God for the vestibule, a crucified Saviour to hang over the altar. The artist was given free reign to sculpt his vision of a Belfast Jesus Christ and Virgin Mary.

I begged for details.

"Can't ruin the surprise," Sean said.

In the vestibule, behind two sets of doors, stood Mary. She was five feet tall and must have weighed 140 pounds. Her brow was thick, her eyelashes were bushy. The Virgin's nose and mouth were prominent and she had broad shoulders. Her dress was formless; her brushed hair was long. Mary was definitely of working-class stock. Too many years in the weaving mill had taken their toll; too many kids to raise; too much fried food.

"She looks sort of Soviet, don't you think?" said Patricia.

"Falls Road," I answered.

Sean nodded.

"Is she the Hulk?" I asked.

"Mother of Hulk," he replied.

The interior was octagonal, with a low ceiling, a tile floor sloping down to the altar, and sections of stained glass wedged into the walls. We found seats in the last pew. Even from the rear, Christ was an extraordinary presence. He dangled over the altar like a Fokker triplane in an aviation museum. The saviour was a pigeon-chested man with tree-trunk arms, sprinter's thighs and the paunch of a Guinness drinker. His hair was long and shaggy and, from where I sat, he needed to shave his neck. On his face was an expression more suited to a reincarnated Buddha than a suffering Jew: an attentiveness and focus, but also a detachment. This Jesus hung on no cross: he *was* the cross. From the back of the church I saw no crown of thorns, either.

"Wow," I whispered.

"Makes an impression, doesn't he?" said Sean.

"He's fat."

"A tub, right enough."

Patricia glanced over at us.

"He's meant to be a figure of power," said Sean, cupping a hand over his mouth. "Someone to watch over us. Protect the church from loyalist bombs, I suppose. So says the fella who carved him, at any rate."

"Shh!" said Patricia.

We fell silent. I fell under the spell of the Hulk: his broad forehead and heavily lidded eyes, his strong jaw and bulging neck. His body, too, was impressive: a thick torso and trim waist, the loins of a Greek god. For a dying man, he seemed potent, energized. He reminded me, ironically enough, of a healthy tree.

"I like him," I decided during the homily. We were all on our knees now.

"He grows on you," agreed Sean.

Patricia frowned. "He scares the children," she whispered, bending over as if to retrieve her missal from the floor. "One or two have complained of nightmares."

"Old people won't even use the front pews," added Sean. "Too afraid he'll fall onto them."

"They're the ones who offer a prayer *before* they go into mass," I said.

Sean snorted back a laugh. I took out a handkerchief. Patricia scolded us with her eyes while her lips quivered.

"The priest looks worried," I said during communion.

"Sweat on his brow," confirmed Sean.

"He keeps . . . he keeps . . . ," said Patricia. She was turning red now. "Looking up . . . to check if . . . ."

I offered her my handkerchief.

"Shh!" someone else said.

Back at the house, I let Maureen pour me a cup of tea. She and James had been to mass the afternoon before; they were planning to go again at noon. I described the church experience in brief, leaving out mention of our being reprimanded for giggling.

"What do you think of the Hulk?" I asked.

"I think he's a grand wee man," she answered. "We get on quite well, he and I."

"Oh?"

"He's someone I can respect. Big and strong, ready to protect but also to fight." She smiled. "I can talk to him. And I do," she added, smiling.

"Not everyone shares your enthusiasm."

"A lot in the parish want him out."

"Out?"

"Of the church. Into the basement. Into the lough, as far as most are concerned."

"What about Mary?"

"Och, that one," said Maureen. "Very hard to warm up to her. So . . . ."

She extended her hands to grasp the right phrase.

"Lumpen?" I suggested.

"She reminds me — I know this sounds terrible — of one of those republican women you see on the television, marching in civil rights demonstrations with their wains strapped to their chests, shouting, "Brits out," and "Down with the imperialists." I never imagined the Virgin Mary to be so *tough*," said Maureen, drawing out the last word in astonishment.

"The hard woman," I said.

"Belfast made her that way."

"You too?"

"I'm tough as they come," she laughed.

Dinner was long over. Presents, removed from beneath a trimmed tree at the rear of the sitting room, had been opened. One gift to the family, a small plastic bird suspended on a long coil, now hung from the chandelier. The bird was red, wore a bowler hat and silly grin, carried a cocktail umbrella under his wing. He bobbed over the proceedings, up and down, up and down. I watched it, despite myself. So did everyone else.

Outside was a miserable night. Whorls of trapped wind in the greenhouse, splashes of rain against the glass, the attenuated ring of the telephone, reminded us of the setting. But the doors were sealed, the drapes were drawn and the fire glowed, emitting a steady throb of heat. Our bellies were full and our thoughts were swimming in liquor and cheer. There was no news to watch tonight. No papers to read.

James Last was back on television. Aengus was back curled like a donut before the fire, with Quixote filling the hole. The air was once again smelling of fur and coal. Sweat was once again trickling down the insides of my arms. Kate, meanwhile, was ruddy-cheeked as a farm girl. She too peeled off layers; she too rolled up her sleeves.

When tea was brought in, the wave of hallway air felt wonderful. When James immediately asked Bernie to close the door, my heart sank.

"Cheers," said Maureen, accepting a cup of tea.

"Cake?" Bernie asked me.

I was bloated, bursting. I put my cup of tea on the table and I thanked Bernie for the slice of cake.

"Doesn't that guy ever move?" I asked, staring at the TV.

"Beautiful music," sighed Maureen.

"Chuck think's he's ill," said Sean.

"Who's ill?"

"Not tonight," warned James, waving his cigarette. "We had plenty of that —"

"I think the man is dead," said Ciaran. "I think they've propped him up on stage with a board."

"Phil Coulter is dead?" I asked.

Mairtin, who had been out the room most of the previous evening, expressed shock.

"Aengus is the sick one," commented Maureen.

Hearing his name, the dog struggled to his feet. For a moment he swayed, and Quixote dashed for cover. Aengus lumbered over to Maureen.

"He's cooking tonight," she said, patting him on the head.

The beast lurched my way. Guessing his destination, I blocked my crotch with my teacup.

"Hot dog," I offered.

"There's a smell off him, for sure," said Bernie.

Kate was next.

"Watch out, Kate," I said. "His eyes are all fishy."

"I'm not actually that fond of —"

The dog reared up on his hind legs and planted two paws atop her thighs. She said "aahh" and spilled her tea.

"He wants a kiss," said Mairtin. "Go on, Kate, give the lad a wee peck."

"Get down, boy!" she commanded.

I heard this: *Giid haand, baay!*

The McNallys heard different.

"Geet ooch, eh!" said Sean.

Aengus, though, heard nothing. He sat, calm and attentive, his snout six inches from Kate's face. Even thinking about his breath made me queasy.

"Doesn't he follow commands?"

"Geet ouch, Eh-gus," commanded Ciaran.

Nothing.

"I think he's puzzled," said Maureen.

"By what?"

There was a silence.

"I don't think the dog really understood you, Kate," volunteered Patricia.

"Speak Irish," I advised.

"You mean my accent?"

"It's quite strong," said James.

"I suppose it is."

"Aengus," said Maureen. "Down!"

Aengus got down. Whimpering, he returned to the fire, pillowing his head on the grate. A chicken would have roasted that close to the flames.

"No offence now, Kate," said James. "I imagine you find our northern accents quite strong."

"Sorry, Mr. McNally?" said Kate. She tugged on her ear. "My hearing's not what it used to be."

Everyone laughed.

"Well done," said Bernie.

"Good on you," agreed James.

Kate beamed.

"Let's ask Chuck," said Maureen. "Are we all, Irish and Australian alike, a challenge to comprehend?"

"Why ask me?"

"Because you're the only one among us without an accent, I suppose."

"I don't have an accent?"

"Not really."

"Nothing at all?"

"You have a little something in your voice," said Sean. "Not as flat and broad as an American. Still . . . ."

I was devastated. "I thought everyone had an accent," I said. "Some are just more pronounced than others."

"Could be," said James diplomatically.

I turned to the other foreigner for support. "I speak with an accent, don't I?"

"Not like this lot," answered Kate.

"Sorry, Kate?" asked Bernie.

"Get down, boy!" I said.

"Pardon?" said several people.

"Repeat what I said, how I said it."

Kate shrugged. "Gaad ahm, oy!"

"Maureen?"

"Och, Chuck. I couldn't . . . ."

Sean could. "Gaat damn, bye!"

Ciaran could, too. And Bernie, and even Patricia.

"See," I said. "You all pronounced my words differently than Kate did."

"So?" asked Sean.

"So I must have an accent."

"So *we* must have accents," corrected Mairtin.

I groaned.

"Sure we're all God's children, Chuck," said Maureen. She giggled to herself.

"Equal in the eyes of the Hulk," added Sean.

An hour later and the door still had not been cracked. Nor had any windows been opened. From the grate came the heat of an open furnace.

Aengus appeared no longer capable of moving, of saving himself. Intervention, agreed both nurses, was necessary.

Ciaran rolled up his shirt sleeves.

"Haul with your arms and legs," advised his father. "Not with your back."

It looked as if Ciaran were wrestling a cadaver. It looked, momentarily, as if the stiff would triumph. Finally, after much grunting and cursing, he succeeded in hoisting the dog up from the carpet. He staggered over near the tree, where he dropped the animal like a sack of coal.

"Good work, son," said James.

Quixote immediately emerged from under the chair to join his friend, and flicked his tail at the dog's head. The dog sneezed. The cat drew nearer. A few minutes later, a still stoned Aengus began washing Quixote with his tongue.

An argument ensued. The topic was Kate's legs. Bernie, an excellent gymnast, maintained that long legs did not grant an athlete undue advantage. Kate disagreed. She loved sports: jogging, tennis, wind-surfing. In all these pursuits, she claimed, her physique gave her an edge. Mairtin suggested a test. Why not try kicking the bird hanging from the chandelier? With Aengus out of the way, a body could elevate, make contact, then land softly back on the carpet. Easy. Harmless. Good crack.

One rule only, added Sean. You had to kick the bird with your feet. No hands.

I assumed the brothers were joking. I assumed the parents wouldn't tolerate such silliness.

Kate went first.

"Easy as falling off a log," she predicted.

The bird dangled a half-metre over her head. She placed herself beneath the target, extended her arms for balance and executed a magnificent scissor-kick. Her left foot thwacked the bird hard, sending him spinning. Her right foot never even left the ground.

We applauded.

Bernie was next. She tried scissoring, but for all her skill her legs were simply too short. Eyeing the target, she smiled and dropped down into a handstand. She then pushed up, smacked the bird with her heel and tucked into a forward somersault. An alert Sean slid his chair from her path.

More applause.

"You people are pole-axed," I offered.

"Now the lads," said James.

In succession, Mairtin, Sean and Ciaran used varied and impressive means to set the mobile spinning and rocking. None landed on his feet; all escaped injury. (Mairtin, though, seemed to favour a wrist afterwards.) The final lad rose from his chair for the first time in hours. My limbs were stiff, my bladder was throbbing. Approaching the bird, I examined its dumb grin and silly hat, the umbrella in its absurdly anthropomorphized wing. A great deal was at stake here, I sensed, especially in the wake of the no-accent slight. At issue was hardly just long legs and athletic skills. At issue was nationhood. At issue was pride.

I was kicking the bird for Canada.

But I couldn't scissor like Kate, and never in my life had I completed a handstand. As for the Bruce Lee manoeuvres of Sean and Ciaran, I foresaw only disaster: a felled Christmas tree, a squashed cat. One option remained. Accepting the consequences, I took a step and flung my legs upward, inverting my body in mid-air. I did not kick the bird; I punted it. I did not land softly back on the carpet; I embedded myself into it like a missile into a beach. On my way down to earth I noticed something fly past me. Landing on my head, with the bulk of my weight pressing the base of my neck, I crumpled — not tucked — into a ball.

"Oh dear," I managed.

"What was that?" asked Patricia.

"The umbrella, I think," said Bernie.

"Well done, Chuck," said James.

I waited for the pain to subside. After a while, I spread out in Aengus's spot, hands corpse-like across my chest, watching the bird swing over me. The conversation turned to other matters. I felt forgotten. Also warm and sleepy. Time passed. A smell reached my nostrils.

"Chuck's cooking," said Ciaran.

Patricia offered to refill my teacup, for when I was ready to get off the floor.

"Dreadful news about Phil Coulter," said Mairtin.

I thought I'd wet my pants.

"It's so nice here," I eventually said.

The same officer who had flagged us down now sauntered over to the car. His swagger wasn't a pose; the man was tall and gangly, awkward in gait. He was also maybe twenty years old. When I saw his stubbly chin and sallow complexion, I decided that we were about to be questioned by a boy. When I glanced at his assault rifle, oddly fake-looking up close but obviously heavy, obviously real, I decided his age didn't matter.

Our car was surrounded. The soldiers before either headlight held their weapons slack, one hand on the barrel, the other on the stock. On the passenger side was a third soldier positioned more aggressively: his rifle pointed at the window — at Mary's head. Anna leaned forward in her seat in curiosity.

The man was so tall he had to either hunch beside the door, an arm slung over the window frame, or else remain a foot back to keep his eyes within the driver's sightline. Wisely, he kept his distance and shouted. "Where are you going?" he asked.

I told him.

"What part of the city?"

I told him. Bluntly. Using monosyllables.

He studied our passports. I studied my responses. What was the matter with me? Our being selected for questioning wasn't the problem. Nor was the incongruity of the roadblock in such a setting all that disturbing. Even the obvious — the insult, not to mention the potential danger of pointing weapons at ordinary people whose only crime was to use public roads — hadn't yet crossed my mind. What rankled, irksome as nails on a blackboard, was the soldier's accent. When he first spoke I jerked my head back in shock. To hear the harsh tones of working-class England, broad and nasal, full of blunt stresses and glottal stops, on a motorway in County Down was for some reason jarring, even offensive.

"Purpose of your visit to Belfast?"

Was this question allowed?

"Lunch," I replied.

"Lunch?"

I repeated my answer.

He scanned the documents again. His fingers were nicotine-stained, his teeth jagged. "Thank you, sir," he said.

The soldier's position was, I knew, unenviable. In a country he probably couldn't care less about. Among a population either overtly hostile to him or covertly ungrateful, full of a strange, obscure spite for all foreign presences, even those invited. Warned to treat everyone as a possible assassin. Considered a legitimate target himself, but rarely having the chance to fight the enemy face to face; far more likely to be ambushed, shot in the back, blown up. In Northern Ireland for a six-month term, the most loathed, lethal assignment in the army. Anxious only to survive. Trying to stay alert. Bored.

"Can we go?" I said.

He nodded and stepped aside, and the sharpshooters lowered their rifles. I crawled ahead, accelerated slowly on the shoulder and re-entered traffic.

"Weren't you friendly," commented Mary.

"They were pointing guns at —"

"I know," she said, cutting me off.

The checkpoint had put our daughter at risk. *We* had placed her at risk by driving into a state where armed roadblocks were routine. But that didn't explain how I had acted. The more I thought about it, the more I recognized that the source of my anger was hearing the soldier's accent on Irish soil. That, however, still made no sense. Ireland wasn't my country. "Brits out" didn't roll off my lips.

I wasn't even hostile towards English accents. I had grown up with them, after all. Willowdale had attracted British emigrants back then, and half our neighbours on Dunview Avenue spoke with intonations. Even I had something in my voice. Over the years I had been often told — especially by my wife's flat-voweled midwest American family — that I pronounced certain words with a lilt, ended some sentences on an up note, used vocabulary aloof from North American idiom. Not an accent, exactly: an inflection, a tone. (The McNallys probably couldn't hear the variation.) I had always pleaded too much time in Ireland, too many Irish friends. What I neglected to consider was a childhood inhabited by adults who spoke different forms of English, starting with certain neighbours and extending to Blessed Trinity School and then Brébeuf College, where I was friends with the sons and daughters of emigrants from Cork and Tipperary.

I had also never considered the effect of having been raised first in a household, and then in a city, where incoming minority languages intersected constantly with the majority tongue. Phone conversations with my mother and her sisters up north were half in French, half in English. English, I noted, was employed to dispense information and share gossip; French tended to be preferred for matters of the heart. Shifts occurred abruptly, often in mid-sentence, but only rarely — as when, for instance, the subject was unhappy — seemed a screen against eavesdropping children. Before I learned French at school, I learned how to piece together narratives by combining what my mother said in her second language with what she implied in her native tongue through gestures and tone of voice.

Meanwhile, part-time jobs at local shopping centres served to introduce me to Torontonians from more wide-ranging backgrounds. Mall superintendents issued instructions to cleaning staff in broken English, then complained about our work in fluent Italian. When they spoke English, all verbs were present active, most grammar was irregular, and intonation was driven by the syncopation of a Mediterranean tongue. Quickly I learned to interpret their commands by adjusting verbs, adding missing words. If those experiences weren't enough to teach practicality and tolerance, there was always Mrs. Giannini. Twice a month our cleaning lady sat down to a sandwich and cup of tea with my mother. Occasionally I joined them at the table for a fractured conversation straight out of Eugene Ionesco. "Chalee nice boy," Mrs. Giannini would offer. "Good boy, go to school, no? My boys, I say: old country no good, new country better, go school, okay? I say, boys, not lika back home, not lika that. Books good: good boys reada the books.

You see?" To which my kindly mother, never blinking, would reply as if there were something to reply to, but would in fact simply start talking.

I enjoyed these lunches, as I enjoyed most encounters with my bosses in shopping malls and my relatives in Blind River kitchens. I liked the bumpy accents and colliding languages and spontaneous neologisms. I even tried imitating speakers: the words they used, the music that shaped the words. I felt no need to correct anyone's grammar or diction; certainly I saw no reason to preach the propriety of standard English. In fact, the only accent that I came into contact with but never mimicked, never internalized, belonged to those strangers living at the top of our street. As a teenager I mocked the *eh*s and *ain't*s and faulty grammar of some Willowtree residents. In the mid-seventies the estate was still largely white, with many small-town people adrift in the city. In a way they were like my Northern Ontario cousins. Up north these were decent, friendly folk, and their ways of expressing themselves were colourful, authentic. Next door to me in Willowdale they became something else, and their English suddenly sounded crude and uneducated, even dishonest. It wasn't the way I spoke the language. It wasn't the speech of our neighbourhood.

CHAPTER V

The word Belfast probably came from *Beal Feirste,* referring to a town at the mouth of a river. Historians disputed the name for centuries; some translated it as hurtleford town, others as a bank of sand.

We approached the city from the south, still stinging from the checkpoint, still not making conversation. The grassy drumlins of Down had receded. Replacing them were a ring of basalt hills to the north and west and a range of smaller, more rounded hills to the south and east. Due north loomed the skyline of Cave Hill. In the middle, straddling the River Lagan, sprawled a city built atop a morass. Belfast sat on wetland composed of silting rivers and sandspits, marshy meadows and bogs. Streams and runoff, trickling down the hillsides, added more water to the basin, further saturating the earth. Belfast Lough was glacier-carved. Silt deposits of eighty metres remained. Old sea cliffs, from when the water level was higher, were still visible along the shores.

Underneath the city lay red sandstone. Covering the surface was alluvial or tidal muck, called sleech. Belfast was built on it. Not on rock, contrary to fundamentalist pieties — on muck. Dig into the earth, and the shovel often turned over sleech. The substance was the colour of claret, and had a unique texture and smell.

Belfast was both built on sleech and — to the delight of poets — built *of* sleech. Brick-fields, their kilns fired day and night, once dominated the cityscape. Literally, the town looked under its feet and found its head; it gazed at the earth and saw the sky. Workers baked sleech into bricks and then grouted the bricks into walls, into buildings and houses, often on the very same spots where they had excavated. The image was potent: a city springing from its own belly, a mud-caked phoenix rising from glacial ash.

Even more astonishing was the recycling process. When the harbour commission decided to landfill parts of the lough, many of those same buildings were taken down and poured back into the water. Slob to slob, sleech to sleech. Queen's Island, where ocean liners were once constructed, was built of dredged-up sleech. The island may have been composed, in part, of mills and shops, of "two-ups, two-downs".

Being half liquid, sleech shifted and slid, settled slowly, if at all. So, consequently, did Belfast. The Albert Clock was a leaning tower, and residences around Queen's University tilted. With houses, the challenge became to establish proper foundations. Older homes definitely listed; older buildings were off kilter. Walls that had once met at right angles now missed, causing cracks; ceilings once horizontal dipped and sagged. In the neighbourhoods nearest the river, like the York Road, terraced houses came to depend on one another. Demolish the end building, and a dozen of its neighbours might creak and groan, even collapse. Wooden braces were used to shore up outer walls. Newer homes were made with imported bricks, smoother than sleech ones, and newer foundations ran deep.

The motorway, built atop the Bog Meadows, was busy, and seemed an ample dividing line between Catholic West Belfast to the left and Protestant South Belfast to the right. I had long ago learned to accept that a neighbourhood in "West" Belfast could be adjacent to, or even south of, one in "South" Belfast. I didn't blink when someone described an area as being in "East" Belfast, despite the map showing it to be south of the south end. Belfast co-ordinates, I now understood, had their purposes.

A massive cemetery loomed up on the Catholic side of the motorway: Milltown, viewed from the bottom. The graveyard flowed down the hill, row upon row of stones and rectangular plots, with empty acres towards the marshy base. As a piece of land, the cemetery was expansive but rough, almost rural. As a site for the funerals of para-militaries, it was dangerously exposed: few trees, lots of sniper roosts. In 1988, a deranged loyalist had killed three mourners attending the funeral of an IRA volunteer. At the subsequent funeral of one of the mourners, a Catholic crowd had dragged two undercover soldiers from their cars and beaten them. IRA in attendance then took the men away and carried out formal executions. Snippets of both horrors were captured by television cameras, and played over and over around the world.

Army jeeps perched on the motorway shoulder below Milltown as we passed. Soldiers leaned on top of the vehicles, their weapons aimed high up into the cemetery at what appeared to be a funeral cortège.

I shifted into the passing lane.

"Turn on the radio," suggested Mary.

The BBC noon news led off with Bosnia. Serb positions around Sarajevo were being strengthened; food and water, medical supplies, were all running low. A Bosnian spokesman deplored the lack of world outrage in the face of the day-by-day, inch-by-inch destruction of his city.

Belfast resolved itself beyond the windshield. The city had no tall buildings; the core was distinguished by the density of Victorian and Edwardian architecture, the impressive green dome of the city hall, numerous church spires. Traffic slowed approaching a roundabout further complicated by a set of lights. The roundabout accomplished what that earlier no man's land could never quite do: it segregated the Lower Falls Road from Sandy Row. Stymied mobs sometimes gathered on opposite sides of the intersection to shout taunts and toss rocks. Drivers had to keep a steady hand as protectiles sailed overhead.

Sandy Row lay a hundred metres from the Lower Falls Road. The Lower Falls Road shared flashpoints, in the form of streets barely wide enough for a car, with the Shankill. The Shankill bled into Ardoyne. Ardoyne backed onto Old Park, onto the Bone, onto Cliftonville. These enclaves were not only positioned on top of each other, but they were all contained within an area so small it could be covered on foot in a couple of hours. Walking, at least, created some distance: a block could be long if the incline was steep or the sidewalk was crowded. Walking also granted each street and shop, each house and flat, a sudden and momentary individuality. These places had character; these residents had faces and names; these houses, however uniform, were all slightly different — a pot of flowers or frilly drapes, a freshly painted door. Of course, a half-century ago the Falls Road was considered a good hike from Ardoyne and an afternoon's excursion from Cave Hill. A century ago people in Falls Road lived long lives without ever crossing the Lagan into East Belfast.

In a few minutes we were north of the Falls, past the city centre and the Shankill and nearing the exit for Clifton Street. I remembered Clifton Street: it fed Carlisle Circus; it was the exit for lower North Belfast. The statue of King Billy, still perched atop the Orange Hall, banished any doubts about location. As we climbed the motorway off-ramp, I braced myself to negotiate the roundabout and navigate the Antrim Road. Anna was now awake again, and rightly fussy — hungry, wet. Mary wanted us to stop.

"To change her diaper?"

"To buy a bottle of wine."

"We don't have to bring anything."

"You *always* bring something."

"Let's buy a cake instead," I answered. "And some scones. Maybe a loaf of bread."

"I thought Maureen kept throwing out stale bread and old cakes," said Mary. "I thought everyone brought them those gifts."

"They do," I agreed. "We should, too."

I entered Carlisle Circus, swivelling my head madly to assess the flow of traffic. Half the cars broke away for the Crumlin Road. I shifted to an outside lane. Antrim Road wasn't posted. But it didn't need to be; while in the roundabout I spotted a landmark, and knew at once where the road lay. From relatively close, the crown of Cave Hill did indeed resemble, as local legend had it, the profile of Napoleon Bonaparte. McArts Fort stood almost 1,500 feet above the soft mud of the Lagan banks. The only direction for us to go was up.

"I'm called Charlie now," I said, sitting before the fire with my cup of tea in August of 1986. "Twenty-six, and already an old man."

"What's that, Chuck?"

"Chuck's known as Charlie now, Mother," offered Patricia.

"You're not?"

I nodded.

"But I'm quite used to Chuck," said Maureen. "Or Cathal, if it's Irish we're talking."

"Have to change with the times, dear," said James.

"I'm not sure I want to."

"There you go," he said.

"I don't mean to pressure you, Maureen."

"No pressure at all, Chuck. I'll just ignore the request. Like so many others I've received over the years," she added, smiling to herself.

"Right," I said.

"But you're still very welcome here," she said.

"Thanks."

"And you shouldn't have brought the *flahhrrs*."

"I know."

"Or the scones," said Patricia.

"You've got a day-old bakery back there in the kitchen," I agreed.

The summer was proving the worst in recent memory. Belfast seemed permanently sullen. No sun, little heat. Winter coal supplies were being pilfered. Fires blazed most evenings. The city was notorious for its eccentric climate: it could be as cold and damp in July as in December; summer rain might be as frigid as winter snow. A morning could jump from late spring to early autumn. Light at noon might be paler than at dawn, while an afternoon would sometimes brighten and warm towards sunset — January to June in an hour. Four seasons in one day. None of them especially seasonable, though; lots of rain, lots of sky. Lots of weather.

Only two factors determined the season in Belfast with any accuracy. One was the length and quality of light. November days were reluctant, a hiccup in the long winter night. May sunsets, on the other hand, often stretched beyond ten o'clock. Darkness, at its deepest, was just gloomy; on certain early summer evenings it seemed little more than a haze. Of course, when there was no sun, days were studies in grey: morning grey, mid-day grey, evening grey. Locals, equipped with hereditary lenses, easily distinguished hues. I saw monotones.

Flowers were a better judge of season. Belfast was marshy, the earth permanently soaked. Infrequent sun notwithstanding, the city could grow anything, tropical or arctic, alpine or sub-alpine, cultivated or wild. Except in the poorest, most downtrodden estates, streets and parks were abloom. Modest row houses managed a windowbox or potted plants on a ledge. Front gardens displayed beds of begonias and phlox, rose and lilac bushes, a fruit tree where space allowed. Ruined houses and vacant lots were overgrown with wild daisies and chickweed.

I had brought a bouquet. Maureen's garden was splendid, her greenhouse a jungle, but I had my reasons: to oblige her to pronounce the word *flower* out loud. No longer a resident of Ireland, I remained a frequent visitor to the island. I had friends there in whose company I felt most comfortable, most engaged. I had fascinations that I now recognized as being rooted in a youthful attraction to cultural and historical paradigms, along with those of language and landscape. The Canada I had grown up in had provided no such models, or at least none that I found appealing. Ireland, in contrast, appeared rich and coherent. Identities seemed solid: people were what they were, not what they weren't. Culture was front-page, important without being boastful, respected. Language was a thrill — almost giddy, almost burlesque. As for the land, it struck me as the essence of a landscape: extremes of earth and ocean, ground and sky. The countryside was wild and awesome and occasionally even perilous, while remaining contained, knowable. It was a land designed for human habitation. Castles and monasteries, dolmens and cairns, were markers of memory and tradition as unerasable as the lines on a face.

Ireland, I decided, placed modest demands on individuals: almost no self-definition or pioneering, and little imaginative engagement with as yet uncharted territories. There was nothing protean about the place.

Race was pure (few immigrants were allowed). Religion was Catholic. Weather was as ever. The North was the North.

In Ireland, you simply chose the stream of your liking — history, literature, music, whatever — and plunged in. The waters weren't dangerous. Other swimmers had calmed them, roped off the deep end, the cold, dark cavities. The pool felt so vast and fathomless. You could swim for ever. Make a career of it, and know a hundred, a thousand others had done so before you, and were people to be esteemed, venerated.

By 1986 I wasn't a teenager any more. I could recognize borrowed clothes when I was wearing them. I could distinguish, a little, interest from commitment, away from home. But I could also identify values that I admired, qualities that I thought worthy, and so I kept returning, especially to Belfast, because it was there I found them most fully expressed: in a sitting room, on a mountain face.

"I've come back to see the new Ireland," I told the McNallys that night.

"Ah," said Maureen.

"Could you be more specific?" asked James.

"The Anglo-Irish Agreement Ireland," I elaborated, mock serious. "Now that all sides are working together in a new partnership. Now that peace is imminent."

James lit a cigarette. I watched him strike the matchbox, fire the tip, then extinguish the flame with one, two, three vigorous shakes.

"Is that what the papers in Canada are saying?"

"Roughly."

There was a silence.

"Who's for a hot drop?" asked Maureen.

I covered my cup with my hand.

"Chuck, I mean Charlie?"

"No thanks."

"A wee drop more?"

"I've already had —"

"Just to warm it? . . ."

I held out the cup.

We discussed the Anglo-Irish agreement for a few minutes, then moved on. After all, except for the moderate nationalist party, the SDLP, almost no one of consequence in the North had even participated in drafting the treaty. The Unionists didn't want a new Ireland. Loyalist paramilitaries were, in fact, killing to preserve the old one. Unionists had refused to take part in the forum; gunmen on both sides weren't invited. On the ground, it was summer in Belfast: Orange marches, riots, murders. Also Diplock courts and supergrasses, shoot-to-kill and plastic bullets.

Our conversation turned to absent children. Mairtin was now married and living in Galway. He worked for an engineering firm. His wife, also from Belfast, was pregnant. Bernie had just left to take up a job in London. Ciaran was in his second year of university in Manchester. Sean, meanwhile, had quit office supplies and recently completed a training program with an Irish relief agency. In a few weeks he would be departing for Bangladesh to help that country improve its telecommunications network. Even Patricia was only recently home from an extended vacation in Canada. She had spent a week visiting a distant relative in Sault Ste. Marie, not far from where my mother grew up.

"Brilliant," she told me.

"Sault Ste. Marie?"

"Such a mix of peoples. Amazing how well they get on, each in their own community, but also living together. I visited a native reserve. It was fascinating."

"The reserve?"

"And the city. The whole country, really."

"She can't stop talking about it," said Maureen.

"Canada?"

"Aye," said Patricia. She seemed almost flushed with excitement. "So vast, Charlie, with so many different regions and different people. It's not at all what I expected. Not at all like here."

"True."

"Such variety. Such openness and opportunity. You make up your life as you go, I imagine: think for yourself, be yourself. A real sense of freedom."

"Go out for walks in your own neighbourhood in the evenings," sighed Maureen.

"The countryside is lovely as well," said her daughter.

"Around Sault Ste. Marie?" I asked, already knowing what her answer would be.

"The forests go on for ever. You can't get through them. No one can. Thousands of lakes and rivers, all teeming with fish and animals. Very few people about, too."

"Sounds different," said James.

"Sounds nice," I said.

"You've never been to where Patricia was?" asked Maureen.

"Not really."

"You're very lucky to come from there," said Patricia.

I nodded.

"Short growing season, Maureen," I added, for no particular reason.

"Bernadette is forever complaining," she admitted. "She can barely get her roses into the ground before the frost comes on. Can't even grow lavender over there, she says. Her *flahhrrs* are often disappointing, Chuck."

"You're very fond of that word this evening, Maureen," said James absently.

"Mad for it," she agreed.

"Lovely place, Canada," repeated Patricia.

We stayed in the sitting room until past midnight. Aengus, a little older and thicker, cooked at the fire briefly, then ambled over to where I sat. He nuzzled my crotch, flopped at my feet. I massaged his belly with my sock. Quixote made an appearance, but preferred to watch birds in the back garden. The Granada, I learned, had been scrapped, not long after being stolen by joyriders and abandoned in a hard-core Protestant area for the McNallys to collect. On the mantel were photos of the children, mostly graduation portraits, plus a shot from Mairtin's wedding. The phone rang twice after eleven p.m. Once the caller was Bernie, the other time Sean. While one parent went into the kitchen to chat, the other studied the corresponding mantel photo. James left the door open when he left. I got up and closed it.

"Drafts," I explained.

"God love you," said Maureen.

On my way back to my seat, I gave the plastic bird, still dangling from the chandelier, a good whack.

With my hand.

I was first up in the morning. Often I would use the silence of the house, the stillness of the city, to slip out the back and wander the neighbourhood, down to the Waterworks, up to the foot of Cave Hill. But Patricia had promised a mountain walk that afternoon. She had even, at my insistence, set an as yet unattained goal for us: McArts Fort, atop the crown. Besides, I had indoor purposes. I began in my own room. The bed I had slept in was sponge-cake soft, smothered in sheets and quilts. Next to it was another bed, two armchairs, a standing closet. In the bay was a dressing table. Decorating the walls were a crucified Christ and a picture of the Virgin Mary with the infant Jesus in her arms. Radiators had hangers to dry socks and underwear. In the corner was a clothes-horse.

My door had kept popping open all night, thanks to a half-raised window that rattled in its frame. Now, I closed the door carefully. It was another sunless morning, and the hallway light possessed no joy, no energy; it shone by rote. Though all the rooms were shut as though on drowsing sleepers, I knew better: two of them were unoccupied.

Even in August, the morning air could be sharp. Usually it was cooler inside houses than outside them. Usually the heat warmed up rooms and corridors just as night fell and the dampness crept back in.

I climbed down to the small landing, rounded the oak newel post, and descended to the main floor. The staircase ran down the centre of the house. At the bottom was another corridor and three more closed doors. The hallway ceiling was edged in plaster moulding and centred by a brass chandelier. The white wallpaper was bordered in green, and delicately patterned. The carpeting was gold. Against one wall stood a polished table-mirror for mail and keys. Above it were rows of mounted china plates.

Flanking the outer door were side lights that narrowed incoming beams. The light then encountered an inner door, its glass top panel decorated with a flower pattern in delicate hues: yellow and rose, eggshell blue. Speckling the hallway floor behind it were diamonds of colour. From the hallway I could hear, but not see, the street outside. Someone walked past the house with a dog. Tires churned water over the pavement.

I opened a door onto a waft of furniture-polish air. The scent was of apples and wax. Dominating the dining room was a table made of oak with an ornately scrolled pedestal. A cloth of intricate lace covered the surface. The table showed signs of disuse: piles of letters and documents, a box of silverware waiting to be polished. At the back of the room stood an upright piano. At the front was a bay window twice curtained: a silk gauze conformed to the window shape; a heavy drape drew straight across the front. The room featured the finest fireplace in the house: tiled, with a dark mahogany mantelpiece. I had never seen the fire lit, and the mouth was filled with weeks' worth of crumpled papers.

Careful to pull the door closed, I crossed to the sitting room. Cinders still cooled in the grate. The scent was so pervasive it almost went unnoticed, like incense in a temple. But the parlour always smelled of coal. The room was nearly the length of the house. The front curtains were gold, as were the walls and carpet, and though light failed to part them, it did seep through cracks. At the rear was a door that opened onto the greenhouse. The light back there was dim.

The room was stately, with a sampler of furniture and ornaments not only from the McNally's previous homes but from the houses of their parents. In one corner was a teak cabinet, in another a hanging cupboard. There were also a mahogany table, two ottomans, lamps with fringed shades, lace doilies and pewter ashtrays, a gilt mirror over the mantel.

At once a formal parlour where guests could be entertained, as well as an ordinary sitting room, this elegant chamber merited a fire most days of the year; was worthy to display photographs of the children; was the only chamber, I sometimes sensed, where family memories met family realities in relative comfort and peace.

Heading down the corridor to the rear of the house, I watched breath vaporize before my face. My hands were pink. My ears were stinging. I needed a cup of tea.

The smaller dining room, off the kitchen, was rarely used. Maureen kept the table extenders down and James had paid to have the fireplace removed. Some ironing was done here, some sewing, and during winter clothes were dried against the radiator and atop wooden racks. In size, the room was similar to the sitting room of an ordinary terraced house. I could easily imagine it serving that purpose: the (restored) fireplace glowing, a couch and chairs pressed up to it, the teapot kept warm on the hearth tiles, a television soundless in the corner. What the sitting room in a West Belfast terrace house would likely possess, however, which the McNally house did not, were decorative icons: the 1916 Proclamation and Irish flag, a Gaelic cross made in Long Kesh. I had never really noticed this before. In this home there were crucifixes and holy pictures, framed prints of Yeats poems and ballads, plus an array of oval family photos, but not a single direct representation of Irishness, of ethnicity.

And yet the house was full of old things: furniture and paintings, statues and vases, family heirlooms from before the Great War. Except for appliances, in fact — the radios and television, the car outside — little in the McNally home looked later than 1969. None of it even appeared to acknowledge the Troubles, down to the wood front door, the flimsy locks, the easily broken windows. No question this was a Belfast house, an Ulster house. No question it was an Irish house as well. But almost all the indicators of belonging were either cultural or else essentially private: associations with a personal history, a class and a religion.

Back in the kitchen with Quixote and Aengus, I debated whether to slip out the door for a walk. Plucking up my courage, I instead made tea for four and carried the tray back through to the landing, up the stairs. Even choosing the right doors was tricky; I had, as usual, gone to bed before the McNallys. Who was sleeping where? I guessed, deposited three cups of tea and knocked softly. Next I sat down on the top step and, warmed by a fourth mug, pondered what compelled me to now mentally map this house with the same urgency with which I had once mapped North and West Belfast.

A door opened. A foot stepped forward. A head, poking into the corridor, gazed down at the mug. A hand reached . . . .

"Ahh," said a sleepy Patricia. She turned to the stairs.

"Shh," I said, placing a finger to my lips.

Patricia withdrew into her room. I felt content. To ask for more would be greedy. But then another door opened. Suddenly shy, I slouched behind the banisters. I caught a glimpse of a white head bending to pick up the cup. Maureen said softly, sleepily: "Lovely."

And it was.

After putting down the phone, James immediately dispatched Patricia to Castlereagh, the RUC holding centre, to see if she could make contact with either Mairtin or the officers who had arrested him. That meant the eighteen-year-old crossing the Lagan into East Belfast, alone in a car, at night. But fears of what might happen to Mairtin in prison — beatings often occurred within the first hours of detainment — exceeded fears of Patricia having to stop, or being stopped, on the Protestant side of the river. Nor could Sean be spared to accompany her. Well known around Belfast was the pattern of swift army raids on the homes of arrested Catholics, ostensibly to gather evidence, mostly to exact revenge. If the army broke down the McNally door that night, it was best that Sean, as next oldest son, be present and accounted for. The house went on full alert. Lights were dimmed and Bernie and Ciaran were tucked into bed. Everyone else stayed up.

By the fall of 1972, the Provisional IRA had evolved from a defender of northern nationalist communities into an aggressive paramilitary organization. Recruitment had climbed after internment the summer before; it soared in the wake of Bloody Sunday in Derry. The break from the Official IRA had been wrenching, and the new group's mandate was, from the beginning, to expel the British army and establish a socialist United Ireland using the tactics of a guerrilla war. Such an approach had, after all, been more or less invented by Michael Collins and the revolutionaries of the 1919–1921 conflict. The IRA had fought a half-century ago to expel the Brits and found the Republic: the goal was basically unchanged.

The acronym itself resonated with Irish nationalists. Associations were part nostalgia, part myth. What shame could there be in volunteering for the army that had once defeated Britain? The original IRA, sabotaged by their own, never had a chance to finish the job properly. The Provisionals would complete it now.

Young men were especially smitten. The rhetoric was pure adrenalin; injustice in Northern Ireland was transparent and outrageous; the solution was obvious, unavoidable. Nor were the Provos yet the secretive zealots of a decade later. Early on in the Troubles, the IRA were, more often than not, your neighbours and schoolmates, the fellas on your football squad, the men you greeted at mass on Sunday mornings. They were people you respected. They were your friends. Often enough they were your own family: a brother or father already lifted, already imprisoned, an uncle or grandparent immortalized in photos and stories.

By the fall of 1972, the Provisional IRA was already shooting British soldiers and RUC officers, bombing pubs and supermarkets, battling security forces in congested neighbourhoods. The organization had also begun exploring other forms of terror, such as knocking on the door of a bus driver who had agreed to testify in court and, instead of simply issuing the man a warning, killing him in front of his wife and children.

The McNally house was not raided; Patricia managed only to confirm that her brother was in custody. Mairtin, caught attending a meeting in a West Belfast house, was remanded to the Crumlin Road Jail to await trial. For six months he was incarcerated in the ancient facility three kilometres down from his house. In prison, he was treated decently: no beatings, no forced interrogations. Though in a state of shock, James and Maureen both visited him there, submitting themselves to the humiliation of having to approach the dirty Corinthian columns, knock on the metal door right out on the busy street, and then be searched. The trial was brief. Mairtin was sentenced to three years for IRA membership, and was transferred to the political blocks of Long Kesh, just south of the city.

Three days later, a van appeared outside the McNally pub in Antrim. Though no warning was called in, suspicious police cordoned off the surrounding block and helped James clear the bar. The bomb exploded at around noon, blowing in the front façade of the Circle, collapsing the roof and bringing the second floor down on top of the main bar.

It happened all over again. Compensation for the pub would take a year; meanwhile, the family could no longer afford the Antrim Road house. This time, there was no discussion of leaving the area. North Belfast was where they lived, where their children were being raised. The McNallys moved into a terraced house off the Cave Hill Road.

All their difficulties aside, the point about remaining outside the ghettos was the same. James and Maureen maintained two hopes: to conceive of a future for their children, and to preserve a family life. They were actually being ambitious. By the early 1970s, many northern Catholics faced a bleak future. Especially in West Belfast and Bogside Derry, where individuals were exposed to a relentless if familial indoctrination into the collective values of their people, and where practical balances to tribalism — a job or house elsewhere, a social network outside the fold, even just the perception of a slow shift in the status quo — were imperceptible, the future didn't stand a chance. People knew what they knew and were comforted by it. What they knew was that, in their neighbourhood at least, nothing changed and the past, a definable insult, a clear oppressor, ruled. What comforted them was that, in their neighbourhood, everyone wearily agreed that nothing changed and the past, regrettably, held sway.

In a real sense, such a mindset made a healthy way of life, with its faith in development and change, impossible. During wars, public schemes and private plans were postponed to deal with the vital moment. It was now believed to be a time of war in parts of the North. In societies where the state apparatus was oppressive, individuals often threw up their hands in despair at ever establishing a personal existence — the proverbial "life is elsewhere" of *samizdat* and Soviet Bloc literature. For ghetto Catholics, the state, both unionist Ulster and England, was an oppressive force, with unjust laws and an occupying army to ensure its hegemony. There too dreams died easily, despair quickly surfaced. Finally, in any place where poverty was dire and prospects were limited, people sought shelter in the imaginative and spiritual houses they had constructed from history — sufferings endured atavistically, memories expanded into legend, feelings hardened into politics.

Up the Antrim Road, however, and in certain South Belfast neighbourhoods, resided another class of city Catholics. Surviving outside the metaphorically walled communities was at once easy and tough. The view from beyond was different; a perspective shored up by more financial security, more inbuilt mechanisms for success, but also by a stronger impulse to coexist, even to interact, if only because these principles were good for business, good for peaceful living. Such impulses boded well for the future: how could Northern Ireland ever work if the two sides did not practise respectful coexistence and at least polite interaction?

For three years the McNallys had to live with the implications of being officially considered "involved" in the Troubles, even if only by association. There were disturbing phone calls from unidentified speakers who wanted James and Maureen to know that *they* knew about their son. These speakers made threats that slamming the receiver down failed to banish from the mind. At checkpoints, their name now came up on lists and in computers. That meant being pulled over, made to step out of the car, pressured to answer additional questions. It meant simply being detained at a roadblock for an hour without explanation. It also meant surveillance of the house and RUC visits to enquire after the activities of the other McNally men. The financial settlement for the pub became complicated; their situation, claimed officials, was special. The prospect of another long wait loomed.

Having a son in Long Kesh also had implications socially. Certain friends cooled to the McNallys; there were sharp words, glances in church, back chat. James and Maureen both suffered. Around Belfast and Northern Ireland were hundreds of parents in similar circumstances, but most of these families were from backgrounds and communities where involvement was more widespread and accepted. The grief might be the same, but not the shock or the stigma.

The Troubles escalated significantly during Mairtin's time in prison. Belfast experienced periods of near anarchy. Bombs or bomb scares rendered the city centre a risky place to shop. Dozens of Catholic-owned pubs were blown up. Devices went off at train stations and bus depots, during church weddings and funerals. Paramilitary groups set up barricades in areas and declared them "no pass" zones; citizens erected debris walls and tea huts to keep out the army and the terrorists. In West Belfast, riots and raids became routine. North Belfast was now becoming the ideal spot for both assassinations and random sectarian murders, including those carried out by the group eventually known as the Shankill Butchers. Volatile demographic shifts continued: Catholics were chased out of the Crumlin Road and Rathcoole. As the displaced poured into the Falls Road for protection, the ghetto expanded up into Andersonstown and the new estates of Twinbrook and Turf Lodge. These shifts, in turn, expelled long-time resistent Protestants. Politicians and judges were shot. Children were accidently killed. Pregnant women were gunned down. Old people got caught in the crossfire.

When Mairtin McNally was released in late 1975, he emerged a harder, toughened twenty-three-year-old. His views were uncompromising; his manner was austere and controlled. The experience had marked him. But Mairtin was not interested in any further involvement, and, typical of northern men, maintained this position with the same stubbornness he had brought to an earlier commitment. Welcomed back into the house, he resumed engineering studies at the Polytechnic. The latest McNally house was cramped and crowded, but also bought and paid for, once the compensation money materialized. Their old/new neighbourhood, Cave Hill, was not a ghetto, not an enclave; their street was still mixed, increasingly a rarity in North Belfast.

The family was even back in the pub business. Admittedly, the operation was more modest than ever: part ownership in a pub in a staunch area of Armagh City. James was being still more practical, still more reductive. Parts of the town were mini-fortresses: a Protestant would think twice about entering these neighbourhoods to pick up a newspaper, never mind plant a bomb. Belfast would seem even farther away down there. He bought, in other words, into a local: a dim, amber-hued drinking hole for men and women who lived around the corner, up the road. Even so, business wasn't great. Too much army harassment of regulars, too many republican clubs around town.

Much had changed, of course. The parents felt the diminishment most: of lifestyle and hope. By the mid-1970s the vocabulary of an older Northern Irish generation had undergone a drastic alteration. People like James and Maureen might refuse to leave the North, refuse to succumb to segregating demographics, might even refuse to give up attempting to earn a living, but they did eventually cease referring to the "current Troubles" and the "present situation". They too were living in just the Troubles, the Situation. It was even, they sometimes had to admit, the Conflict, the War. Their children's vision of the post–August 1969 world might have been alienated, even cynical, but it had also proved correct.

Patricia and I set off for Cave Hill shortly after lunch. The day was once again grim and the sky was a pot lid. The mountain fit just beneath the rim: our view was unobstructed the whole way up. Aengus came along, officially on the leash I kept wrapped around my hand. Being granted his freedom did not translate into aggressive behaviour. The dog sniffed lampposts and wandered up front walkways, but otherwise puttered along at our side, not so much obedient as listless, tired.

"His form hasn't been good lately," admitted Patricia.

"Form" was the eldest McNally daughter's measure of well-being. Patricia's standard opening — "How's the form?" — paralleled Mairtin's "What about you?" and Sean's "What's the crack?" If over the years I assigned too much underlying meaning to these greetings, each McNally child did seem to be asking a slightly different question. Patricia appeared most concerned about health. Was everyone happy? In a good mood? If not, then there was a problem. Perhaps not one easily solved, but addressing it frankly, openly, could only help.

She was, after all, a nurse. An excellent one, apparently, with years in North Belfast emergency rooms and several periods of study, including the winter in Scotland, to enhance her skills. Patricia's holiday in Canada had put her in a reflective mood; she had an aunt in Toronto who could sponsor her application, and several provinces were so short of nurses they were promising to help with visas. If she wished, she could apply to immigrate tomorrow. In six months she could be an employed (and well-paid) resident of St. John's or Sault Ste. Marie or Calgary.

Patricia was now thirty, and the last child still at home. Her commitment was in small part to Belfast, in large part to her parents, whom she adored. She had Maureen's round face and hushed voice, James's clear eyes and brilliant smile. She blinked frequently when she spoke, as if counting her thoughts; like her father, she often held a teacup aloft while composing a sentence. A thoughtful person, she tended to be slow to speak, more comfortable in one-to-one situations, where her cadences wouldn't be drowned in the uproar. In group settings, she opted more for listening, laughing in the standard McNally manner — high and hearty, rocking back in her chair.

We had been making excursions up Cave Hill for seven years now. Among the McNallys, Patricia was the least athletic — a little golf, no gymnastics, certainly no football — but also the most avid walker. Our route was established: we would head north along noisy Antrim Road, then cut in through streets of detached homes to the entrance to Belfast Castle. Though not as scruffy as in 1979, the mountain remained largely untamed. Woodland trails were well trampled but less well kept: strewn with garbage, overgrown. The castle, boarded up for years, was under renovation. We angled across the mown grassland below it, past the ornamental planting and specimen trees, to where the trails to the caves began. From the foot of the hill we could still see the suburbs squeezed between the mountain and the motorway, the cranes and oil containers of the dock area, the lough. We could compare, at my insistence, the two dominant ingredients of the city's distinctive smell, in force after a night of rain.

Coal always formed the base. When it was being burned, chimney smoke obliterated all other scents. The odour was acrid; to the North American, accustomed to the sweet fug of wood, it reminded one of machinery, hot engine grease. Coal smoke smelled of miners smeared in grime, towns choked in smog. It smelled of train travel, of the nineteenth century: Dickens's London, Monet's Paris railway stations. Coal smelled of the past, of a past when cities were industrial engines and humans residing within them were cogs. A smokestack- or gantry-backdropped urban landscape of row houses, their laneways crowded with dustbins and bikes and sagging clotheslines, their sheds bursting with fuel, the path to the kitchen door smeared black—that landcape could only be accompanied by the stench of coal.

But the dominance of coal in Belfast was challenged by the fragrance of cut turf and bog. This was especially true on Cave Hill. The smell of rural Ireland blended with the smell of industrial England. Turf was used in fires in both the Republic and rural Ulster; some cutting went on in the hills that surrounded the city. Burning turf gave off more a taste than a smell. Belfast might be all coal, but it was situated in lowlands, shadowed by hills, surrounded by farmland. Rain soddened the earth, soaked the vegetation. Sunlight then extracted scents, as if from a cake baking in the oven.

"You haven't noticed it before?" I asked.

"What?"

"The smell."

"Everyone says the city smells of smoke," agreed Patricia.

"What does smoke smell like?"

"Belfast, I suppose."

The woodland quickly bowered us in foliage. On the steeper inclines our speech became curt and breathless; hands were pressed to thighs for the extra push. Aengus trotted ahead or else vanished into the woods, often scaring up commotions of birds. The silence was uncanny; except for a faint hum I recognized as the motorway, no urban sounds reached us. Cave Hill was tiered. At the bottom unfurled the small manicured landscape surrounding the castle. That terrain was dominated by hazelwoods and planted gardens. Higher up lay the woods Patricia and I were making our way through. Spread out above the tree line were bracken- and bluebell-carpeted moorlands. Finally, there was the bald rock face of the crown. Fulmars reeled over the promontory. So did sparrowhawks and peregrine falcons. Below, tree branches held the nests of kestrels and robins. Badgers and even the rare fox called the woods home.

A couple with a dog descended the path. I unravelled the leash to feign exerting control over Aengus. He, happily, had disappeared. The other dog was a yappy terrier; the couple were older, dressed for a rainy excusion — tweed caps and wellingtons. We all exchanged greetings. It was a soft day, wasn't it? The weather was only miserable this summer. The view from the caves was grand indeed.

In Belfast it was still considered impolite not to acknowledge someone you passed on a pathway or along a quiet road. (Pedestrians in the city centre were exempted.) Equally, however, most formal rules for social exchanges were disavowed. At-home murders had become commonplace around town. Sometimes the assassins would sledge-hammer down the front door in the middle of the night, storm upstairs and shoot the victim in bed; on other occasions they simply rang the bell and waited for an answer. Despite the terror, in many areas neighbours still left outer doors open in the evenings, a traditional sign of welcome. Despite the terror, many people still took any form of screening to be rude, uppity. Enquiring who the caller might be from behind a door, peeking through a sitting-room window, inserting a keyhole or insisting on clear glass: these measures smacked of self-importance and conceit. Belfast wasn't like Dublin or London. The city didn't have a serious drug or crime or murder problem. Locals were proud of the general calm that pervaded, the general decency displayed — except, of course, for the crimes and murders and (increasingly) drug deals made because, and in the name, of the Troubles. People were proud of their town's code of sociability, of calling in to friends without warning, of leaving doors open and locks unlocked, of offering a hello or a good afternoon to strangers on a secluded mountain path.

"The parents have lived here their entire lives," Patricia was saying. "It's their home. They've never known any other."

"And you?"

"It's a bit different. When you're younger you can conceive of starting a new life. You haven't those attachments, those memories, to hold you to one place. You can *see* yourself somewhere else, I suppose."

Patricia used the second person singular when talking about herself. She also gazed straight ahead, too modest to meet the other person's eye. She too would expect friends to appear unannounced. She too would think it rude not to answer a knock on a door.

"Can you see yourself moving to Canada?" I asked.

"Absolutely."

"You must look fetching in a wool cap."

"Fetching, Chuck?"

"A colloquialism," I answered. "I'm full of them."

"I never noticed people using that many odd or unusual expressions over there. At least, none I hadn't heard before. Not like here, or in Australia."

"We borrow the language of others."

"I'd still emigrate at the drop of a hat," she said. "Or a wool cap."

"A tuque!"

"Excuse me?"

"We don't call them wool caps. We call them tuques. From the French, I think."

"Only in Canada?"

"You bet."

"*To-oo-kk*," tried Patricia.

"You must find my accent difficult," I sympathized.

The light brightened up ahead. Once out of the woods, directly beneath the caves, we stopped to slow our pulses and prepare for the equally arduous — and never yet completed — trek around the face of the summit. The McNally house and neighbourhood were hidden to the south. Visible below were the reclaimed land of the dockyards, the most northern metropolitan suburbs, including the concrete towers of Rathcoole, the entire Antrim coast to Carrickfergus and a horizon of Irish Sea. The Mourne Mountains were in mist. Scotland remained obscured. But the landscape close by, especially a few kilometres due north, was already cast back in the verdant idyll mode: patches of fields and farmhouses, grazing sheep and cows.

"With Mairtin and Sean and Bernie and even Ciaran gone," resumed Patricia, "I feel a little bit the homebody, you know, still on Leeson Avenue, still in my room."

"It's a great house."

"I feel very comfortable there."

"Stepping out the door? . . ."

"Exactly, Chuck — I mean, Charlie. Stepping out the door starts the problems."

"Sean says he feels lighter outside the North," I offered. "Less put upon. More free."

"It's known as post-traumatic stress syndrome," said Patricia, in a rare foray into medical terminology. "Being in the place where it occurred usually makes treatment impossible. You're too involved, too caught up. Once you step outside, you feel more at ease. But it doesn't mean you're over it. It doesn't mean you're free."

"Just lighter."

"Aye."

We were silent for a moment. The wind spat water at us; I could see my own breath.

"What about Aengus," I said. "Think he's suffering from trauma? Think he's a Troubles dog?"

Her answer was postponed by a burst of grrs and yelps. Aengus, we both muttered aloud, was back on the prowl. Climbing a path that wound up towards the lower caves, we called to the dog. The caverns were mysteries: definitely man-made, but for unknown reasons. (The largest cavity, up near the fort, may have housed prisoners.) They were small and shallow, good for little except beer and cigarette parties, awkward sex. Many *appeared* accessible, and people had been killed trying to scale the vertical face. The caves certainly lent the mountain an eerie aspect. From the city, they resembled empty eye sockets.

Suddenly the dog bounded over a rise. He went straight to Patricia and, to my surprise, rubbed against her leg.

"Must have met a bear," I said.

Patricia, ashen-faced, was looking past me. She was also extending a polite greeting. Turning, I found two men standing on the rise with their hands in their pockets. Both were young and black-haired. Neither had shaved that morning. Neither smiled.

"How's about ye?" asked one man in a thick accent.

"Fine, thanks," I answered.

"The leash, Chuck," said Patricia. She was holding Aengus by his collar.

"What?"

She turned her eyes to the leash still in my hand. Quickly, I unravelled it. Quickly, Patricia harnessed the dog.

"We're on our way," she told the men.

"Good day."

We wished them a good day, too.

The path resumed nearby. I counted to fifty before either looking over my shoulder or speaking. The men had vanished. The rain teemed.

"They didn't look like beer drinkers," I commented.

"Indeed not."

Once around a bend, we stopped again. The view should have been of a smaller hill across from us, with the distant suburb of Glengormley along the valley floor. Except that the clouds were now disintegrating down onto the estates and apartment blocks. The world beyond the tree line was about to be enveloped.

"We have to keep going," I said.

"Why's that?"

"Because we've set out to reach the fort before, and never made it."

"It's not much, to tell the truth. Just a few stones. You might be disappointed."

"There's a point to reaching the top," I mumbled, blowing air into my hands.

Patricia smiled. "Tell us," she said.

"You know . . . ."

"I don't think I do."

"Wolfe Tone and Henry Joy McCracken. The United Irishmen. Men meeting in caves to plot insurrections. That stuff," I added, uncomfortable at the prospect of having to explain my latest half-baked theory.

"Like those men back there?" asked Patricia.

"Different."

"Go on."

"You *know*," I repeated.

"Maybe I don't."

How could Patricia not know? The United Irishmen were a rebel group whose botched 1798 rebellion had haunted the nationalist imagination for almost two centuries. The uprising was planned and launched in

Belfast; leaders held secret meetings on Cave Hill; Wolfe Tone pledged to fight for Ireland's freedom up near the fort. Though supporters of the oppressed Catholics, and proponents of a thirty-two-county republic, the United Irishmen were, in fact, largely Protestants, especially in Ulster. A particular brand of Protestant, though: Jacobins drunk on the French Revolution, democrats intoxicated by Thomas Paine and the new United States, and plenty of anarchists and atheists willing to sup on anything that might undermine British authority. Tone was a lawyer, McCracken a businessman. Other leaders included a doctor and a librarian. Members indulged in lengthy dinner parties, loud arguments, drink. They sought emancipation for Catholics, equal treatment for all Irish and liberation from king and empire.

The rebellion was easily crushed. Belfast was riddled with informants, and after a few desperate and uncoordinated attempts at insurrection the principal leaders were rounded up. Wolfe Tone, captured in the west while trying to land a French fleet, committed suicide in prison. Henry Joy McCracken was arrested on Cave Hill and hanged in a square in the city centre. Others received perhaps stiffer punishments, sentenced to live into old age observing the discrediting of Presbyterian liberalism in Ulster and the gradual emergence of what would become the Orange state.

Though himself Protestant and anti-imperialist, Wolfe Tone became the first in a long line of heroes in an increasingly nationalist and Catholic nineteenth-century insurrection. In the name of Wolfe Tone, men and organizations like Robert Emmett, the Young Ireland Movement, the Fenians, the Irish Republican Brotherhood and the IRA pursued a course of physical-force republicanism. Their politics might be rooted in lofty Enlightenment ideals, but the United Irishmen unwittingly left a legacy of a mythic and inward-looking agenda: violent, socially retrograde, Catholic. Membership became bred in the bone, in the hair colour, in the family name.

Nonetheless, in the ecumenical make-up of the United Irishmen, historians saw a model of consensus; in the progressive ideas of the group, a vision of a non-sectarian state. In their purposeful anti-imperialism, with its emphasis on egalitarian principles of government, intellectuals saw a miracle in Irish history — a reconciliation of communities, a moment of synthesis — perhaps capable of being repeated, certainly available as an example.

The ideas weren't mine, of course; many scholars and intellectuals held the United Irishmen up as exemplars. My half-baked contribution to the discourse centred on the physicality of Cave Hill. First, I granted the mountain the status of emblem: it embodied those two-hundred-year-old ideals. Then I volunteered the observation that, no matter where you lived in Belfast, the mountain was starkly visible. If not from your sitting-room window, then from your front door; if not from your front door, then from the street corner.

Patricia listened patiently, once or twice pulling on the leash to keep Aengus on course. The weather had further deteriorated. The air now had a bite, and the wind was a faulty shower faucet hurling splashes of rain in our faces. Visibility was also on the wane; the pass between two landslips we had to reach, straight ahead five minutes ago, was now lost. Cloud tails brushed the moorland. Wisps of smoke shimmied across our path.

"What do you think?" I finally asked.

"We'd better turn around."

"About my theory?"

Patricia paused for so long that I wondered if she preferred not to answer. "Do you support the IRA campaign of violence?" she asked finally.

"Of course not."

"But didn't Wolfe Tone lead an armed rebellion?"

"Not the same."

"A lot of people in this town wouldn't agree," she continued, blinking her thoughts. "They use the United Irishmen and other instances from history to justify bombing pubs and shooting people in their beds. They think it's the same situation, the same cause."

"I'm focusing on other qualities of the group — the respect for individuals, the fairness."

"Right enough. But Tone and his friends were still determined to establish this wonderful republic by the blood of British soldiers, and most likely of a lot of innocent Protestants and Catholics, too."

The level voice, the insistent questioning, the suggestion not so much of underlying contrary views but simply of a suspicion of speculation and conjecture; even gentle Patricia adopted the McNally manner when the subject was politics.

"But the principles . . . ," I pleaded.

"Lovely, I'm sure," was her reply. "I was raised to cherish them, so I was. At school we were taught almost nothing else. These men and women were our heroes. They would point the way to a United Ireland. A good northern Catholic education," she added quietly.

I fell silent.

"You're robbing me of my moment, Patricia," I finally said.

She laughed. We turned around.

Back near the caves, now masked in fog below and in cloud higher up, I scoured the broom for the men. Patricia, I noticed, shortened Aengus's leash. Once back in the woods, we were better protected from the rain, except when I jumped up and yanked on tree branches, producing brief but violent showers. Aengus barked after the second time, and I stopped. The downpour had muted the scent of meadowsweet on the crown. But in the sheltered woodland the air was steamy and pungent, the perfume a blend of soaked earth, tree bark and vegetation. The murmur of rain on leaves buried the motorway sounds. The city just beyond the trees, just down the slope, retained a presence thanks only to the dogged tang of coal, like cigarette smoke in clothes.

"I've a question for you," said Patricia. "You said before that Cave Hill was visible from all over the city. Have you spent any more time in East Belfast or down below the university than we have?"

"Not much," I had to admit.

"Why not?"

I told her about Mairtin's car tour back in 1979. Less the details, more the Belfast map: how he had outlined for his cousin and me a city west of the Lagan, shadowed by the Antrim Hills. How the parameters of that three-hour tour had, I realized afterwards, encompassed only a small part of the city but nearly all the major hotspots, the key flashpoints; how, for a Troubles watcher, Mairtin's Belfast had been dead on — where the conflict was, would likely always be. And how realizing that the map was both incomplete and exclusive still hadn't done much to broaden my focus.

She repeated her question.

"Because of your family," I answered.

Patricia frowned.

"I know I should meet more Protestants and get to know other areas of the city," I said. "I know my perspective is narrow. But . . . ."

We stopped on the path.

"Yes?"

"I guess I've taken sides."

"Why do that?"

Should I tell her about the house? The sitting room? The closed doors and cups of tea and roaring fires? "Maybe it's natural," I answered feebly.

We walked in silence.

"Maybe," I added a minute later, "I need to."

The rain stopped two blocks from the house. Never could I recall being so wet or so cold. In my weakened state, all my anxieties about the McNallys' safety surfaced. I felt deep in my skin the magnitude of the Troubles, the complexity, the tangle. I shivered at the prospect of having to sort through this mess day in, day out, while remaining sane and dignified, not to mention hospitable. I doubted I would be up to the task. I doubted I would even want to test myself that way.

"You look the picture," said Maureen in the kitchen. She had been in the garden, weeding.

"We nearly drowned, so we did," answered Patricia.

"Who's for tea?"

"Please," I said.

"A scone?"

"You bet."

"Biscuits? Fruitcake?"

I smiled.

James, busy working on an article in his bedroom since morning, appeared.

"Chuck — I mean Charlie — is going to follow Sean and live abroad," offered Patricia.

"Are you?"

"I'm thinking of trying to get an international teaching job," I said.

"Any ideas?"

"Asia or Africa. Maybe India."

"We could enquire of the priests over at St. Malachy's if there are any openings," said James.

"Och," said Maureen. "Chuck's after something exotic. A real experience. Aren't you?"

"North Belfast would be an experience."

"It surely would not," she replied.

"An experience of *what*, I'd like to know," said James, laughing.

"If those other places don't work out, I'll give you a call," I promised.

We brought our tea into the sitting room.

The Willowtree Estate didn't go away, except that children from the original families grew up and scattered, and our block on Dunview Avenue didn't go away either, except in the same manner: parents staying while their kids drifted off to colleges, jobs, other cities. Eventually I moved downtown to attend university, returning home for Sunday dinners and the occasional overnight stay. I would get off the bus at the corner of Church Street and Willowdale Avenue, but would now cut through the estate to our house. Walking along the paths, past the never-filled pool and brimming dumpsters, the cramped back yards and squinting windows, I could only shake my head in disbelief at my childish fears of this harmless place. How ordinary the apartments were, how ordinary the people who lived in them, how ordinary — in all likelihood — were their lives. Ordinary, I now understood, like the homes on our block, the people in our homes, the lives we led.

Sometimes the face of a man or woman around my age would register, and we would exchange weak smiles of recognition. These were the boys and girls who had been raised up the road from me. They had drawn hopscotches on the cement at the elbow of Dunview and Longmore; they had tossed frisbees and baseballs on the field beside the basketball court. Later, they had trundled off to the local public high school, though many hadn't finished, and had wound up being the teenagers who broke windows and blared Kiss records and roared up the street in fast cars. At different periods of my youth I had lacked for friends my age in the neighbour-hood. These kids had been right there; still, I had never played with them. A year could go by without our even sharing a word. I didn't know who their favourite hockey player was, what they thought of Rush or Supertramp, if they ever went to games at Maple Leaf Gardens. I didn't know which buildings they lived in, who their parents were, where they had come from originally. I didn't know their names.

Our block had put a metaphorical mile between us and the Willowtree Estate. We had pretended great distance where great prox-imity existed. Consciously or not, we had decided on the need for sides, and chosen them, and then ensured that few crossovers would be wel-comed. I had been raised in a segregated environment. Not only from the families of the Willowtree, either, but from neighbours on the block whose class, religion and simply inclinations were different from — and occasionally at odds with — our own. None of this was out of the ordinary. No malice was intended; parents wished no one harm; their only concern was safety and comfort for themselves and their children.

What was extraordinary was how long it took me to recognize that Dunview Avenue and Willowdale were like everywhere else. We hadn't escaped history after all. People hadn't checked their pasts at the bor-der or on the exit ramp off the 401. People hadn't been born again merely by settling onto a new street in a recent neighbourhood in a postwar suburb. Difference and distinction, which I had thought existed only in the privacy of living rooms, had in fact been spilling into the roads: in what we thought of certain neighbours, what they thought of us; which families we mixed with, which families mixed with us. Just because the human impulse to segregate hadn't resulted in terrible social problems didn't mean it wasn't present. Only we had been negotiating common ground, dancing around difference, with more success than people in countries where there was little ground to negotiate and less room to dance.

And there was nowhere else for us to call home. No England or Ireland, no Blind River or Ottawa. Though it wasn't presented that way, Dunview Avenue was our community: where we came from, where we belonged. The language that was "ours" was simply the words and expressions we used to describe our experiences. The accent was just the way those words came out. This being Canada, both the words and the accent were simultaneously old and new, rooted and transient — an accurate reflection of history past and history ongoing. What we made of it all, how we conceived of ourselves as individuals within history, families within a society, constituted all the actual degree of belonging, the actual sense of community, that we could ever establish. Our houses were last houses, too.

The McNally house was only a kilometre away when I stopped the car outside a bakery across from the Waterworks. I had planned to buy just a cake or a flan, but then I noticed flowers on the sidewalk of the newsagent's next door, and went over to examine them. The bouquets of carnations seemed fresh; their scent was crisp, almost sweet. In a minute I was back in the driver's seat with a cake for everyone and *flahhrrs* for Maureen. Mary made no comment.

Just above where we were parked stood the junction of Antrim Road and Cave Hill Road. Either would carry us up into the McNallys' neighbourhood. I chose to stay on the Antrim Road, to scout for the Hong Kong–run hotel and pub near the turn-off. The BBC was still discussing Sarajevo; I clicked off the radio. Though the hotel had vanished, the pub was open. I found the road but then somehow lost my bearings. Briefly I imagined we were in the wrong place. Homes were still elegant, streets were still quiet, but the neighbourhood seemed deserted. Few people were about; all dogs must have been chained. The sky had darkened again. Cave Hill, when it abruptly ballooned over the houses, was aloof and brooding. No one, I now accepted, could live up there.

The smell of coal was dispiriting.

I had to ask directions. We were already on Leeson Avenue; the house was just a block farther north. Reversing, I drove towards a figure standing on the sidewalk with its arms crossed. It was James, smoking a cigarette, his arm a pendulum. He waved me into the driveway.

"We're here now," Mary soothed our daughter.

James butted his cigarette on the asphalt. He welcomed us warmly. "We were getting worried," he admitted. "Did you have any trouble finding us?"

I shifted my gaze to Maureen on the front steps. Her eyes were fixed on Anna, whose middle name had been chosen in her honour. Anna, in turn, glanced over at her mother for instructions. While she climbed down from the back seat, and Mary greeted James, I examined the house, a sturdy, not-too-crooked structure certain to outlast the McNallys' occupancy of it and, most likely, the occupancy of the conflict in the city. The house seemed immortal, unchangeable. We, in contrast, were all looking just that much older.

"No trouble," I assured them both, checking my voice for cracks. "I know where you live."

PART II

Now as news comes in
of each neighbourly murder
we pine for ceremony,
customary rhythms:

the temperate footsteps
of a cortège, winding past
each blinded home.

from "Funeral Rites"
Seamus Heaney

Almost every night that I am in Belfast in September 1993, and again in May 1994, to research this book, an ordinary citizen is killed by a paramilitary. Most of the murderers are loyalists, engaged in a particularly vicious campaign aimed at derailing the first rumoured, and then confirmed, peace negotiations and subsequent IRA ceasefire. I learn about the assassinations watching the television in the McNally sitting room, listening to the radio in the McNally kitchen, reading one of the half-dozen newspapers James now has delivered each morning. Sometimes I pass by the site of an incident on a walk, and stop to examine the house where the victim was sleeping, the construction site where he was working, when masked men came up and shot him. I study the police cordons, the armoured vehicles by the curbs, the staring kids and not-staring adults. I shield my brow with my hand to glance up at the helicopter ratcheting above the neighbourhood. I lower my gaze to passing foot patrols. Locating the murder sites isn't difficult; half of them are in lower North Belfast, within twenty minutes of the house. Twice I follow a funeral cortège up the Falls Road towards Milltown cemetery. Once I come upon the procession by accident; the other time I plan my day around meeting it.

I considered renting a hotel room and simply ringing the McNallys, maybe dropping by for tea. The distance would have been beneficial. James worries when guests stay out after dark. Maureen appreciates a call during the day. What researcher works with a curfew? What journalist calls home at lunch?

I stay with the McNallys. I have never spent a night in Belfast except within their walls. I have never thought of the city without thinking of them. I ring Maureen at around noon each day to inform her of my movements; I return each night before dark.

When I arrived, I was astounded by the quiet. Only James and Maureen occupy the house now. Half the rooms are in disuse. Half the doors are permanently closed. Curtains stay drawn; dust is left to thicken on presses and tables. My first evening there, Maureen handed me a stack of fresh towels. I asked which room I should take.

"You can have the pick of the lot," she answered.

The quiet is comparative. Back in Montreal, my wife and I share an apartment with Anna. We keep each other up most nights with feedings and insomnia, work deadlines and bad dreams. We are too familiar with each other's rhythms and personalities; we are a family now.

In a way, I am just like the McNally children: I drop by for a few days, maybe a week, and then return to where I actually live. I inform James and Maureen of my plans, recount my itinerary, but often alter details, leave out segments, that might alarm them. I have my own sense of Belfast, my own rules about safety and propriety, risk and result. Not only am I from a different country and a different past than the parents, I am also from a different generation.

We are watching the BBC Northern Ireland news in the sitting room. The fire is low, the teapot is cold. James sits in his chair next to the mantel. Maureen and I share the couch. The lead item is a murder: a forty-eight-year-old mother of four, Teresa Dowds de Mogollon, has been gunned down in her house in Fortwilliam Park. De Mogollon was

reading her daughters a bedtime story at around nine o'clock when the
bell sounded. She descended the stairs. Her front door contained
frosted glass; to see who was calling, she had to open it. Before she
could turn the handle, gunfire shattered the glass. Her daughters found
her in the hallway.

The UFF has admitted responsibility. Her husband, Peruvian-born
businessman Max de Mogollon, was the intended target. The organization "deeply regrets" its error.

Maureen smoothes the arm on the couch, repeatedly, as if it were a
cat's spine. James lights another cigarette.

"Who's for more tea?" she asks.

"Lovely," answers her husband.

"You, Chuck?"

I smile.

The news moves on to the war in Bosnia.

Maureen has been in my room. The curtains are drawn and the bed-
clothes have been turned back. On the endtable is a small pitcher of
water with a cloth over its mouth, and a glass. There is also a book for
me to read, an anthology of Northern Irish poetry. I look at poems for
twenty minutes. Soon the house, and the street outside, settle into the
preternatural calm more common to sleepy towns than bustling cities.
Sounds are amplified: a dog barking, a child singing in her room, a
footfall on asphalt. The sky is more purple than black and the moon is
a blur. I smell coal, and rain, and Cave Hill. A breeze billows the curtains like a clumsy intruder.

The afternoon paper leads with a brief report on the murder of Jimmy
Bell, a driver for a food-supply company. Bell, in his late forties, was
approached by two men while unloading his van at an ice-cream factory
in East Belfast. They shot him repeatedly in the chest. Bell was killed,
reports the paper, because he was Catholic. Following up on the de
Mogollon murder, another newspaper notes the rise in sectarian assassinations of Catholics and refers to North Belfast as the primary "theatres
of operation" for Protestant paramilitaries in search of an easy kill.

The city centre is looking sharp these days. The security checks are long gone; some stores hire guards to check handbags and briefcases. Vehicles still aren't permitted in the central core, except buses and delivery vans, meaning the wide streets are pedestrian thoroughfares. Belfast now has a Gap store, an HMV, a Waterstones; it has fancy shopping courts and self-service cafés. The sidewalks are cleaner, with more benches and trash bins, more unvandalized telephones. Still lots of men selling lighters to support the IRA, though; lots of art students sketching St. Sebastian on the sidewalk with coloured chalk; lots of ruddy evangelists enquiring of shoppers if they know where they will be after the final judgement.

Statistically, there are fewer bombings than ever in the city centre. Statistically, it is safer down here than any time since 1969. But the RUC continues to check vehicles, jeep patrols continue to rumble up the streets and helicopters continue to hover overhead. Nor is there any getting used to the sight of combat troops in a narrow lane packed with mothers pushing prams, old ladies wielding shopping bags. The soldiers appear to be in the wrong movie: a mistake of scheduling or location. Some seem to feel that way, too. One afternoon I catch a soldier lagging behind his patrol. He is staring into a shop window, his back to the street. I study his reflection in the glass: he looks stiff and uncomfortable, imprisoned in a flak jacket and helmet, khaki pants and black boots. He also looks bored. The store sells sporting equipment. The soldier, perhaps dreaming of furlough, examines a pair of Nike cross-trainers on sale for fifty pounds sterling.

Maureen tells me about Aengus's final days. The dog was so far gone he couldn't stand up or see beyond a few feet. After he spent a winter indoors, Maureen finally steeled herself and brought him to the veterinarian. The doctor gave Aengus an injection, then left the two of them alone in his office. Maureen sat on the floor beside the dog and wrapped her arms around his neck. She soothed him until the end. Then she wailed for ten minutes, out of control, inconsolable. She was a wreck for a week afterwards.

Quixote passed away the previous spring. The cat lived to be nineteen, a life undistinguished by achievement, uncluttered by incident. He was buried in the front garden, and his kitchen basket sat untouched for months. Finally James folded up the blanket and stored the basket in the shed. Maureen still hoovers up cat hair.

On the mantel now are more and different photos. School portraits have been replaced by wedding shots. Children vie for frames with grandchildren. Mairtin is the father of two boys and a girl. Bernie has a baby boy. Sean, only recently returned to Ireland after five years in Asia, lives with his wife in Cork. Ciaran works for a company in London. Patricia, meanwhile, sends letters and postcards home from Calgary, where she is a senior nurse in a hospital. When the phone rings late at night, which it often does, James and Maureen no longer have to rise, open the door and hurry back to the kitchen. A gurgle sounds from the cordless stand beside James's chair. He waits a ring, then picks up. His voice fills the sitting room with laughter. At the other end, his children may hear the roar of the fire, the TV, a siren outside. They may even be able to close their eyes and re-create the sitting room: the quality of light, the variety of smells, the sensations — of warmth and security, unease and dread — particular to Belfast, to their childhoods. Maureen meanwhile fastens her gaze on the mantel the whole time her husband speaks. She strokes the arm of the couch, smiles at his questions and their presumed answers, the general banter, the crack. When he hands her the receiver, she begins by softly addressing her child by name.

The evening news is bad. There is more about Teresa Dowds de Mogollon, some footage of the van Jim Bell was driving, a report on two Catholic construction workers shot in the Shore Road and an update on a huge IRA bomb that destroyed a suburban supermarket. Ian Paisley appears on screen to denounce the bombing. John Hume appears on screen to denounce the rise in sectarian assassinations. Hume, the younger man, looks worn and tired; Paisley, over seventy, is vigorous and intense.

"It could be 1979," I say, marvelling at the staying power of these figures.

"Try 1969," says James. "Sure, those two have been at it since the beginning."

"Paisley looks good."

"Too mean to die," sighs Maureen.

"Hume seems old."

"The best age quicker," she says. "Am I not right, James dear?"

"No argument there."

On my way up for the night, I mention an article I read in the *Irish Times* concerning the GAA. The RUC recently found a cache of arms in a North Belfast GAA club, prompting loyalist paramilitaries to declare the association an official enemy. Anyone associated with the GAA in the North — players and coaches, journalists, even fans — would now be considered a "legitimate target" for retaliation. Had James heard about the threat?

"Aye," he answers.

Maureen sighs again.

Careful to close the door behind me, I go to my room.

The next day, I try to intercept the funeral of Teresa Dowds de Mogollon. A newspaper mentioned that she would be interred in Milltown. Not by chance, I encounter a cortège exiting St. Paul's Church, across from the Royal Victoria hospital on the Lower Falls Road. The flower-ribboned hearse is already in the street, blocking traffic in both directions, and a dozen men in grey and black suits are carrying a coffin down the front steps. A smaller, dowdier crowd than I expected forms a procession behind the pallbearers. Faces are old and haggard; no children grasp at hands.

Passers-by stop, remove hats and caps, bless themselves. I lean against a wall. When a man gives me a look, I quickly raise my right hand and brush the bridge of my nose with three fingers. I slide the hand down my chest, make contact, then advance to the left shoulder and the right. The last time I made the sign of the cross was at Christmas mass in a church on the Cave Hill Road.

"Good morning," says the man.

The walk to the cemetery is uphill. Encountering the cortège so early throws me, and I hesitate to trail it the length of the road. A block beyond St. Paul's, and the procession has already ceased garnering much notice. I am surprised the de Mogollon children are not present. Nor can I locate Max de Mogollon, whose twisted face as he embraced two of his daughters at the requiem mass the day before made the front page of the *Belfast Telegraph* ("Terror Stalks City" read the headline). His face, her photo, the photos of the children, have not left my mind. Unlike at the mass, though, even the media have kept away this morning. I dawdle behind the cortège for two more blocks, twice more blessing myself to deflect suspicion. Few of the elderly mourners look to be likely friends of a Fortwilliam Park housewife. Few of them look to hail from that part of Belfast.

I slip into a coffee shop and hide my embarrassment behind a newspaper.

Up near Milltown, across from Falls Park, I am stopped in my tracks by an aroma of flowers. The fragrance overpowers the stench of exhaust fumes and the tang of cut grass. Beds in the park haven't yet bloomed and the cemetery is untilled. For a moment I am puzzled, charmed. Then I notice a shop next to Milltown that sells funeral wreaths and bouquets. From its door wafts a thickly sweet smell. Later, this happens again on the Crumlin Road. I am near the jail, and seek out the source. Sure enough, another floral shop. Garlands for inmates: gifts for incarcerated husbands and sons.

Before dinner, Maureen shows me her garden. The evening is soft and the clouds are high. Cave Hill is resolved in the light; the promontory is dove-grey, the green of the woods so dark they look almost in shadow. The light in Belfast is often ethereally bright, the air unnaturally distinct. The sky, especially after a rain, can sometimes appear transparent, a gauze cloaking another sky above it.

Though the McNally back yard is small, it contains a garage and patio, and Maureen's garden. A decade of planting, fertilizing, weeding and watering has paid off; the two beds are a riot of colour and smell.

At the elbow of an L stands a small apple tree. Though the tree bears fruit, the apples are good only for cooking. Around it are bushes of drooping roses and swaying red-hot pokers, dahlias and marguerites, petunias and sweet peas, rhododendrons. The garden has fern and heather bushes, stalks of montbretia, a small eucalyptus tree from California. While I admire the flowers, Maureen bends over her herbs with a pair of scissors. At her disposal are lemon balm and southern-wood, basil and dill, sage and fennel. Tonight's chicken will be sprinkled with basil; the potatoes will taste of dill.

We eat on the patio. Shortly after we sit down, a helicopter positions itself in the sky above the house. The thwump-thwump of the propellers isn't really loud; it isn't even really a noise. The sound is more a hum, muffled but clear, innocuous but grating, like a freeway a few blocks from your home.

"They can hear every word we say, apparently," offers Maureen, shielding her eyes to the sun. "Hello, Mr. Army Helicopter Operator!"

James, obviously irritated, sips his wine.

"Can they see what's on the table?" I ask.

"Right down to the spuds," she answers. "Boiled or baked — they know for certain."

"The helicopters were supposed to reduce the number of road blocks," says James. "They can read number plates from that height. Check who's coming and going from a neighbourhood. Track suspicious vehicles."

"Are there fewer road blocks now?"

"Aye."

Maureen sighs. "They want to see and hear everything that goes on down here," she says. "Know everything about this place. They seem quite obsessed, don't they? I never realized we were so interesting."

Giving up, we clear the table and retreat to the sitting room for dessert and tea.

The evening news is worse. Even Bosnia gets just ninety seconds. Jim Peacock, the Crumlin Road prison guard murdered in his Oldpark home last night, is the lead item. Peacock, aged forty-four, had finished watching the nine o'clock news and was fixing himself a cup of tea when UVF gunmen smashed down his front door. They shot him in the back, in his kitchen, repeatedly. His thirteen-year-old daughter was upstairs reading a book. She cradled her father in her arms.

Peacock's murder was only the worst incident in a night of terror for city prison officers. Some had their garages bombed, their cars blown up. Others were shot at in their bedrooms. All the victims were Protestants living in Protestant areas; all the attacks were carried out by loyalist paramilitaries upset at the treatment of their imprisoned comrades. Jim Bell was mentioned, and Teresa Dowds de Mogollon: three civilians murdered in three days. Also, five children left semi-orphaned.

I call Montreal. Mary, seven months pregnant, is alone in the apartment with Anna. They are reading a book. No need to ask the title: *Goodnight Moon*, by Margaret Wise Brown, still Anna's favourite bedtime story. *In the great green room, there was a telephone, and a red balloon, and a picture of* — I hear the door buzzer in the background. Mary hands the cordless receiver to our two-year-old. Before she does, I ask her — she knows, anyway — to step onto the balcony and see who it is. While she's away, I continue to recite *Goodnight Moon* from memory, and Anna, not in the least surprised that I can read over the phone, turns the thick cardboard pages. Muffled voices crowd the line, and I tense. It would be twilight in Montreal; who could be at the door? My memory stumbles. *Goodnight moon. Goodnight cow jumping over the moon. Goodnight . . . .* My wife comes back on. A neighbour has brought a bag of clothes too small for her own child. Anna screams in delight at the new wardrobe.

She also complains about a boy in her play group. His name is Andrew. "Andrew said hard words today," she says. "The teacher made him sit out."

"Really?"

"He's a hard boy."

"Did he say those words to you?"

"Andrew's a hard boy," she repeats.

My father would call home during the dinner hour whenever he was out of town on business. I think about those conversations in my room in the McNally house. Father was often away in Kingston or Montreal or Calgary or Vancouver; he would usually be back in the morning; late in the evening; in a couple of days. All three kids would be handed the receiver to say hello and then good-night. I sometimes stayed on the line to summarize a hockey game I'd played or a history class at school. Though my father wasn't a big hockey fan, he attended thousands of practices and games over the years to please me. Though I was initially indifferent to history, I studied hard, and excelled, to please him. Now, when I call him up, the subject of our conversations is usually neither hockey (which we both watch) nor history (which we both read avidly). The subject is most often family: he and my mother, me and my wife and kids. I share with him how hard I sometimes find it being a parent. I admit that I miss the girls when I'm out of town, and worry irrationally, absurdly, about what might happen to them in my absence.

James and I walk down to the shops. The elder McNally is now almost seventy. He is still trim and fit; I have to hustle to keep up with him. At the shops he greets everyone by name, enquires after the health of a girl named June in the bakery, the fortunes of an aspiring actor named George in the off-licence. He gets June to smile, George to laugh. He engages in chat, in banter: a bit of the crack. He is polite and gracious, and is, in turn, treated with almost fawning respect. There is a proper way for these exchanges to occur, a decent Belfast way, and James is a determined practitioner of it. Semi-retired, he is a lifer in his home-town, even though we walk past two never-visited Protestant pubs and James admits he can't recall the last time he was in a bar himself. The aura about him is undiminished.

Cave Hill is now a "country park". In 1989 the city became almost sole owner of the mountain. Belfast Castle, home to a restaurant and bar, is a favourite spot for wedding receptions. An adventure playground for kids draws crowds on weekends. Paths are well kept. Signs indicate destination and distance with such accuracy that getting lost would be difficult. McArts Fort is clearly indicated, and I reach it one evening in barely an hour. Patricia McNally was right: it is basically a pile of stones. (The view, however, is beautiful.) Most of the graffiti have been removed from up around the caves, though the caverns themselves remain inaccessible and dangerous. Strollers or joggers barely glance up at them as they pass below.

Michael Edwards, aged thirty-nine, was murdered in his house in Finaghy Park, South Belfast, shortly after midnight. Two UFF gunmen kicked in the front door, climbed the staircase and shot Edwards as he lay in bed with his wife. His six children, aged eighteen months to nine years, were sleeping in adjacent bedrooms. Several of them witnessed the murder. Edwards owned a sweetshop in Catholic Glen Road and had only recently moved into the house, located in a mixed neighbourhood.

The *Belfast Telegraph* runs a front-page photo of the family. The parents are dressed formally, for a wedding or perhaps a first communion, and are a handsome couple. Three boys and two girls stand before them, with the baby sitting proud in her father's arms. Above the photo is the headline "Ulster's new wave of violence". Other newspapers are more dramatic: articles are titled "Terror Walks the Streets" and "Catholics on Alert". In an editorial, the *Irish News* advises Catholics to take precautions when outdoors, especially in unfamiliar neighbourhoods. The newspaper also suggests that people ensure their homes are secure.

The murder more than doubles the number of Belfast children deprived of a parent: eleven in five days.

Maureen is on the phone with Bernie. She sits beside me on the couch, the receiver pressed to her ear. The subject, I gather, is sleep: Bernie's new boy is up as often as four times a night. Though I could share a story or two, I am chatting with James. Like the parents, I am also glancing at the photo of Bernie, the baby in her arms, atop the mantel.

"Do you know anyone who's been threatened?" I ask James.

"Within the GAA?"

I nod.

"You hear rumours," he admits uneasily.

I nod again.

"It's completely ludicrous," he adds, making sure Maureen is absorbed in her conversation. "They're just games, so they are. A way to keep fit, to keep youngsters occupied. And Protestants are fond of the GAA as well. The football and hurling matches get massive ratings on television."

The doorbell rings. It is past ten o'clock; the darkness outside is absolute. I find an excuse to follow James into the hallway. From where I stand, the narrow side-lights offer up no clues, no shadows.

He opens the inner door and switches on a light. Then he pulls the front door open. I watch James peer into the night in puzzlement. After a moment, he glances down. I hear a small voice.

"Right you are, Liam," answers James. "Very kind of you to ask first."

A neighbourhood boy has lost his soccer ball somewhere in the McNally front garden. "Imagine that," says James to me. "Out training even after dark!" He is clearly pleased.

Later, I check the door behind the kitchen. The upper half is sectioned into rectangles of thick etched glass. Pulling the door open, I reach around outside with my hand. The shape before the glass is blurred; my appendage could be a tree branch, a weapon. A knock on this door, too, and the McNallys would have to open it to see who is calling.

"I've come back to see the new Ireland," I say, sitting on the couch with my tea in May 1994.

"Och," says Maureen.

James lights a cigarette with a plastic lighter. Though more efficient than matches, it just isn't the same.

"The day the Downing Street Accord was signed," I continue, "a Canadian newscast said that 'peace was breaking out in the Northern Ireland'."

"Peace?" asks James.

"That's what they said."

"So you've come to see the post–Downing Street Ireland, have you?"

"Right."

"You might have a hard time finding it."

"We haven't, so far," adds Maureen.

We sip our tea.

"How's the new baby?" asks Maureen.

I have photos handy.

"She's lovely."

"Great sleeper, too," I say. "Wakes up only once a night. Sometimes she sleeps right through."

"God love her."

"And Bernie's little boy?" I ask.

We shift topics to grandchildren and children, new houses in Cork and Galway, new businesses in London. After all, the Downing Street Accord, launched by the Irish and English prime ministers in December 1993, has so far been sidestepped by almost everyone in the North, except — as ever — John Hume and the SDLP. The Sinn Fein "studied" the document for months. Then they issued a request for "clarifications" from London. James Molyneaux grudgingly went along, but Ian Paisley's response to consensus building was unequivocal. He denounced the accord as a "sell-out".

The bird dangles from the chandelier. Eleven years later; in the exact spot where I kicked it. The plumage is still red and the bowler hat is still silly. The umbrella is still missing; the spring has rusted ochre. While Maureen is out of the room, I examine the artifact.

"Quite the warrior," I say to James.

"We've had that bird for ages."

"Where's its umbrella?"

"There's a story to that," he laughs.

James repeats the tale of the kicking contest, minus my participation. I don't bother mentioning that I was present. It was so long ago.

The evening news begins with a report that two Catholic construction workers have been murdered at a building site in North Queen Street, just below Duncairn Gardens. Eamon Fox, aged forty-four, and Gary Convie, aged twenty-four, were having lunch in their car when paramilitaries opened fire with machine-guns. Both men were from a small town in County Armagh, and are described as respected members of their community, active in the local GAA club. They commuted up to Belfast because of the job market; on weekends they drove home to be with their families. Fox leaves a wife and four children, Convie a companion and a young son.

The UVF claim the murders.

U2's *Zooropa* is the big hit this spring. The HMV shop on High Street has a wall display of the CD; videos of Bono and the rest of the band lipsynching the song "Stay (Faraway, So Close!)" against a Berlin backdrop flicker on a dozen floor monitors; another book on the group is for sale in Waterstones. Their music is still compelling but now also clowning, almost self-parody. Themes include pop-culture trash and media-induced numbness. In 1991, Dublin was designated the European City of Culture, and was suitably decked out: manicured parks, repaired benches, telephones that worked. Belfast, battling the rap as a hopeless muddle, a self-absorbed backwater, is also attempting to transform itself. The city has some fancy shops and decent restaurants. Certain pubs are posh; night clubs are popular again. Hotels bombed repeatedly keep opening back up with promises of better service, tighter security.

I ask Maureen about the Hulk. There was a purge at the Church of the Resurrection. The Virgin Mary was shunted from the vestibule to a side altar, where parishioners wouldn't be obliged to confront her simply to attend mass. The Hulk suffered far worse. He was taken down from the ceiling, wrapped in cloth and banished to the basement, like the statue of a deposed dictator. In his place is a smaller carving. This Jesus Christ is an emaciated man with a defeated body and a dolorous expression. A crown of thorns drips blood down his cheeks. Nailheads sprout from his palms and crossed feet.

"I miss the old Jesus," admits Maureen.

"What about his replacement?"

"Och, he's so tiny and sad, Chuck, I mean Charlie. There's no fire in him. I really haven't anything to say to that wee man."

"Do other parishioners feel the same way?"

"They do not," she answers. "I'm in the minority. Nothing to be done about it at this stage, I suppose."

Each evening, I bring a cake or scones or a loaf of bread back to the house. I do this despite the fact that the McNally breadbox is perpetually bursting. I do it, in a way, because the box is so full. Maureen routinely picks up a sodabread or a half-dozen wedges of potato bread in the mornings. James returns from the shops with white paper wraps of scones and farls, sweet pancakes and sausage rolls. A loaf of sliced batch is always on hand. When a child is home, wholewheat bread is kept as well. Guests, meanwhile, even those dropping in simply to lend a videotape to James or collect Maureen for golf, come bearing gifts: more scones, more farls, more bread. Alone in the kitchen, I quietly shove hard sodabread or scones into a corner to make room for my own fresher contributions. If necessary, I weed out the old and the stale.

"That's the guy whose wife died," I say one evening. We are watching an American drama on TV.

"Who?"

"That guy. I forget his name. His wife fell off a boat."

"Who fell off a boat?" asks James.

"Y'er man's wife," answers Maureen.

"Y'er man?"

"The actor," I clarify. "In real life, he was married to a famous actress. She drowned accidentally."

"The woman on television?"

"No, his wife."

"She is his wife."

"Not on TV," I explain. "In life."

"And she drowned?" asks Maureen.

"I'm not following," admits James.

"Chuck's saying this," offers Maureen. "Y'er man on the TV show was married to that very same woman, also on the television. Isn't that right?"

"Not quite," I say. "Anyways, I can't remember his name. Or hers. But they were married. Until she slipped and fell off a boat."

"They play investigators or some such thing," says James, blowing smoke from his nostrils. "I haven't a clue what their names are."

"Either do we, dear."

An actress appears in the next scene.

"Poor thing," says Maureen.

"She's not dead," I point out.

"Not tonight, at any rate."

"They're police types," repeats James. "Nothing at all to do with ships."

"I think she was in West Side Story," I add.

"What was her name?" asks James.

"Och," says his wife.

"Y'er woman," I say.

"I ran into Mrs. Keane in church this afternoon," says Maureen, wisely changing topics.

"Who?"

"The elderly woman over on Cedar Avenue. The one whose husband has Alzheimer's."

"What's her first name?"

"That's just it," explains Maureen, trying to keep a straight face. "I couldn't for the life of me remember. It was dreadful."

"How so?"

"Well, I imagine she gets enough of that at home."

"Enough of what?"

"Ach, James."

"Natalie Wood!" I say.

"Sorry?"

"The woman who —"

"I think Mrs. Keane's first name is Mary," offers James.

"I'm called Charlie now," I say.

"More tea?" asks Maureen.

I spend afternoons in the Linen Hall Library on Donegall Square. The library first opened in 1788. Originally called the Belfast Reading Society and located on Anne Street, it was a local expression of the great late-eighteenth-century drive in Western Europe for improvement of both self and society. Members embraced the radical principles of government embodied by the American and French revolutions. Henry Joy McCracken joined the society in 1794. Thomas Russell, another co-founder of the United Irishmen, was appointed head librarian that same year. Dozens of other members of the Belfast Reading Society were secretly associated with the proscribed group. By 1796, with a French invasion of Ireland believed imminent, British authorities began arresting radicals. Manhunts around Belfast invariably ended at the doors of the library; Russell was arrested in his office, and many other members were detained. By 1798 McCracken had been hanged, Russell was still in jail (he would be released in 1803, but executed shortly afterwards for his part in the Robert Emmett uprising) and the United Irishmen were finished. Only the calming presidency of a fiercely anti–United Irishmen merchant saved the society from extinction.

On New Year's Day 1994, the IRA planted a bomb in the library stacks. The building might have burned down had there not been trucks close by, attending another blaze. Outrage at the bombing was so great that the IRA apologized, claiming the bombing had been the error of a nervous volunteer.

The Linen Hall collection contains thousands of rare books and documents; in certain areas, most notably traditional music, it has no equal as an archive. But the two-storey library is a firetrap. Banisters and shelves, desks and chairs are all made of wood; books and folios, maps and musical scores are pure paper. The library moved to Donegall Square in 1892. The premises are cramped and musty, muggy in warm weather and damp in cold; more than fifty visitors, and the place is bursting.

The Linen Hall Library has always been run by Protestants. As an institution, however, it has never been considered the exclusive domain of that community. It welcomes new members; in recent years it has welcomed anyone to simply walk in and wander, do homework, drink tea. Linen Hall is a public Belfast house. Two centuries after its inception, the library remains the greatest, if not the only, example of a city institution that is imaginatively owned by all citizens. Author after author in book after book sings the praises of this modest place. Politics have not been explicit there since 1798. Implicit, however, in the endurance of the Linen Hall are the politics of sanity and principles: principles not of a republican-style government, but of fairness and tolerance, acceptance of difference; politics not of a United Ireland, but of a shared Irish culture and history, a shared vision of the future that excludes gunmen, hard men, bigots.

I feel comfortable in the library, among these old books and faded documents, maps and paintings; most of all, among these people, ranging from students in school uniforms to elderly men wearing double-breasted suits and carrying pocket-watches. The atmosphere of openness and ease, of slight disshevelment and determined calm, even the aroma of polished wood and tea brewing in the café, reminds me of another Belfast house where I also feel welcome, at home.

Maureen drives me to the Ardoyne to visit a family friend. The trip takes us up the Crumlin Road, past the jail, past where the Mountainview stood. The entire block that surrounded the pub has been levelled; the mills are either empty shells or else are being sectioned into rental units; the neighbourhood James grew up in has vanished. Farther along the slope of Divis Hill, she turns onto Ardoyne Avenue. The outing marks her first time back on these streets in years. We end up chatting about the early 1970s, and about Mairtin. Even after two decades, Maureen still struggles to understand how her eldest son, a soft-spoken and kindly man, could once have been such a strident, angry young adult. She sighs and asks, timidly, the question posed to me ten years ago by Mairtin himself. In the same circumstances, in the same frame of mind, would I too not have become involved?

"In your son's position," I answer immediately, "yes, I would probably have become involved."

"You're not just saying it?"

"It's the truth."

She sighs again.

A terrible lie, partially atoned for.

Driving past a park, Maureen names the different flowers on display near the gate: roses and lilacs, a row of oleander bushes. I tell her that Anna fell in love with hibiscus flowers during a recent trip to the southern United States. Actually, she fell in love with their name: high biscuits, she called them. Maureen laughs. "High biscuit *flahhrrs*," she repeats.

I enjoy talking about Anna and her new sister Claire, and miss them even after just a week. Maureen knows the feeling: she and James are away from Belfast more often than they're home — visiting Galway or Cork, flying over to London. James will chat GAA with Mairtin's oldest son for a half-hour on the phone; Maureen insists Bernie put the receiver near the baby, so she can hear him coo. She misses her children and grandchildren terribly. She doesn't wish any of them to come home soon.

The news that evening includes mention of two Catholic teenagers murdered in a taxi office in Armagh City. Gavin McShane, aged seventeen, was killed instantly when gunmen sprayed the room with bullets, but his friend, Shane McArdle, remains on a life support system. His parents have just agreed to donate his kidneys; the machine can now be switched off. There is also a report on secret talks between Unionist politicians and loyalist paramilitaries aimed at ending the current murder campaign. An adjunct story, which I read in the newspaper, is astonishing. A month before, some UVF volunteers decided that they had found a Catholic woman in a loyalist band hall in East Belfast. The men took it upon themselves to beat the woman and then shoot her. When it turned out she was Protestant, a mother of three, the paramilitaries were dismayed. So were their elders; the member who pulled the trigger was himself executed by his comrades.

But the opening item of the nine o'clock news banishes these other reports. The camera is inside a room in the Children's Hospital at the Royal Victoria. On the bed lies three-year-old Emma Anthony. She was in her car seat the week before when an IRA bomb, strapped under the family vehicle, went off. Her father, a cleaner at a police station outside Belfast, was blown to bits. Her mother and brother were both injured. Emma was blasted out the rear window and landed eight metres from the car. Both her legs were broken. Shrapnel lodged near her brain. The girl has been in a coma for seven days, and doctors aren't holding out much hope.

Her aunt has invited television cameras into the hospital. She wants the IRA to see what they have done. She wants to "melt the hearts" of the terrorists. The girl lies on her side atop a pillow decorated with animal drawings. Emma has red lips and long eyelashes. Her breathing is regular; her mouth is partially open. Tubes come out of her nose and IVs sprout from her arms. Her head is shaved, her face is puffy and her tiny body is lacerated with scabs and scars.

We sit stunned. James keeps glancing down at his cigarette, over at the telephone. Maureen keeps rubbing the arm of the couch. Neither has seen anything like it on local television, ever. I have never before watched a two-minute news segment that rendered me at once furious and physically ill, fighting tears. I make stupid, bathetic connections. I can barely hold on until the end of the newscast to call Montreal.

Fixing tea in the kitchen afterwards, I confess to James that, to my surprise, I am sleeping well in Belfast. The cool air, the soft bed, the quiet — I can't help myself. He is amazed. Certain of his own children, he admits, home at Christmas or Easter, have trouble falling asleep in their own beds, their own house. They keep hearing noises outside. They can't help feeling edgy. Maureen mentions that a few years before, Ciaran, having just finished a book on the Shankill Butchers, called up from England to inform his mother that he intended never to set foot in Belfast again. Happily, he got over the shock and now visits his parents regularly.

For the first year of my older daughter's life, I dreamed most nights that she was in bed with us, under the comforter, being smothered. Anna slept in her own room from the beginning, but my subconscious kept transporting her to our bed. Only half awake, I would bolt up and rip off the comforter, heave pillows across the floor. Convinced the child was nearby, pinned down, unable to breathe, I would call out her name, shake Mary in desperation. Sometimes I'd roll off the mattress to check under the box spring and in the closet. Often I could only fully exit the dream by tiptoeing into the nursery, waiting until my eyes adjusted and confirming that the girl was sound asleep, her favourite doll pressed to her chest.

I have the dream in Belfast. Pulling myself out of it, I climb from the bed, murmur to Mary that I'll go check Anna and make for the door. It is wide open; the thin window-drape billows. The odour of coal acts as a smelling salt, and I stop dead. First I pour myself a glass of water from the pitcher. Then I cross to the window. Calming the curtain, I gaze out. The street is deserted. In front of the house an animal, most likely a Black Dog, ambles from bush to bush. At the centre of the silence is a hum. The sound is faint, almost interior, like the ocean inside a shell. The hum grows louder, more distinct: *thwump, thwump*. I scan the sky. I open the window and stick my head out, as if the helicopter might be perched on the McNallys' roof.

From a distant point of blackness, of empty night sky, comes a shaft of light. It is as sudden and miraculous as an Old Testament spectre. The search beam is pencil-thin at the point of departure but widens as it funnels downwards. I cannot see the place of impact from the window. I can, however, watch the beam scan a block of terraced houses or track a car. I can imagine experts in the helicopter, equipped with infra-red goggles and high-powered filters, studying faces and reading licence plates from a half-kilometre over the earth. I can even guess the cause: rioting in Protestant areas because of what reports are calling "unease over the Downing Street Accord". What I cannot believe is that the beam isn't another dream, another imaginary peril or hypothetical intruder. That it is real. How things are here. Have been for a quarter-century. Will continue to be for the foreseeable —

Back in Canada, in Toronto, I ride the subway up to Finch station and walk the six blocks to my old neighbourhood. The Willowtree Estate is tidier than I remember it. Residents are even more diverse now: people from the Caribbean and Africa, Pakistan and India. Dunview Avenue too is in flux. My parents moved out in 1985. At least our house, one of only three clapboards on the block, still stands. Other bungalows and storey-and-a-halfs are gone: sold during the late eighties boom, then torn down to make room for the popular "monster homes". The other house on the block that I knew best, the Murrays', has just been levelled; I watch as construction workers pour the foundation for a residency that will be as wide as the lot. My parents attended a farewell party for the family. Some neighbours are still there, some are gone. A few passed away; most simply went away, as did the Forans.

The street is narrow. The older houses are small. The house where I grew up seems inconceivably tiny, though the trees out front are as vaulting as I imagined them to be as a boy. I remember a great deal about living in this place, and almost all the memories are gentle, fond. But I feel no nostalgia for it. I feel almost no attachment. The new home owners have different faces, different accents. The new residents have different kinds of names. The stores on Yonge Street now cater to Chinese and Caribbean and Arab shoppers. This neighbourhood isn't the one I knew. Music is still being played inside Willowtree apartments, though. Lawns are still being mown the length of Dunview Avenue. Driveways boast two cars and abandoned bicycles, overturned skateboards. Cats sleep on windowsills. Empty baby carriages wait by garden gates.

EPILOGUE

THE CEASEFIRE

On August 31, 1994, the IRA announced its first ceasefire in almost two decades. Six weeks later, a coalition of loyalist paramilitary groups, having failed to lure the IRA back into the fray through further sectarian murder and a bomb on a Dublin train, also declared a cessation of violence. As this book goes to press, the ceasefire, endorsed in late October by British Prime Minister John Major's visit to Belfast, is holding; constitutional politics appear the new order in Northern Ireland.

Sinn Fein's Gerry Adams acted as spokesman for the IRA. For more than a year, Adams and SDLP leader John Hume had been masterminding a pause in the quarter-century-old stalemate, Adams' tone of triumph notwithstanding, the ceasefire represents the failure of the IRA armed campaign: twenty-five years of insurrection, and no results. In July 1994, the Sinn Fein leader reiterated the objectives of his party: "British toops must go, Unionist veto must go, Partition must go." In December 1994, British troops are still in Northern Ireland. In December 1994, Northern Ireland is still a "Protestant" state; by voting as a block, Unionists can effectively (and democratically) veto nationalist aspirations. As for a United Ireland — or at least the traditional republican vision of a United

Ireland — it remains a destructive fantasy. The island has long been par-titioned, and the removal of an already invisible border will not alter that visible fact.

The current ceasefire, then, represents a sea-change in neither the IRA's agenda nor, in all likelihood, its attitudes towards violence. It is probably strategic. If the process stalls, nationalist paramilitaries may seek to resume their old campaign. Their loyalist counterparts, one suspects, will gladly join them back on the battlefield — i.e., the streets of Belfast.

Nor is the ceasefire itself without risk. Commencing negotiations when neither side has shown any inclination to examine old antago-nisms, never mind to revise cherished goals, invites a backlash. (In both Israel and South Africa, where breakthroughs have occurred, the need for changes in social and political structures was more mutually agreed upon than appears the case in Northern Ireland.) Strategies that don't work are eventually abandoned. Worse, they become discredited, as do the ideas that compelled them, creating even harder lines, bleaker prospects for compromise. Similarly, the so-called "fatigue factor" behind the ceasefire, a somewhat cheery reading of the paramilitary mind, also has limits. Tired, disillusioned terrorists regain strength or else give way to fresher faces. Enmity is a powerful stimulant, and for an extremist there is no pick-me-up like the sense of "betrayal" that would result from the failure at a negotiated settlement.

Nevertheless, peace has broken out in Northern Ireland. Does this mark the end of the cycle outlined in the introduction to *The Last House of Ulster*, and embodied in the title itself? Nothing would please me more. But my title was also intended to highlight another quality of the Troubles. Though the complexity of the situation is daunting, the scale of it is not. Northern Ireland remains, to a great extent, the old province of Ulster: one-fifth of an Atlantic island. It is a homey, homo-geneous place where faces are familiar and distrust of outsiders nearly equals that shown towards adversaries. A place where, in certain minds, the very lack of differences between people somehow makes highlighting those distinctions seem all the more urgent. A divided household, in other words, but a single household still. The moment of truth for the ceasefire may come when a document is put forth that obliges the occupants of the various rooms to acknowledge that the future, if not the past, will need to be grounded in equality and power-sharing. Legislated equality; constitutional power-sharing. Put more blandly, family members will have to agree to lay aside conflicts and share a common table. They will have to listen to each other. They will have to show mutual respect.

In Northern Ireland, as in so many other unhappy places, a pessimist is not often proved wrong. Nor, however, is he ever of much help. A few weeks into the ceasefire, this pessimist called the McNallys from Montreal. Patricia was back home to do graduate work. Belfast was greatly enjoying the easing of tensions, she said. Ironically, what she had noticed first was the reduction in the number of surveillance helicopters; the mechanical hum, so hard on both thought and sleep, had receded. British troops now patrolled in berets rather than helmets, and in the countryside they had stopped smearing themselves in camouflage. Downtown shops had relaxed security; guards no longer blocked doorways to inspect bags. West Belfast was still army- and RUC-ridden, and the IRA was using the ceasefire to "clean up" its turf in the usual brutal manner. Still, Patricia declared the city calmer; everyone — including her parents — was breathing more easily.

I asked her how long the ceasefire could hold. To my surprise, she wondered aloud if the IRA could ever resume its armed campaign. The organization has always counted on the tacit support of the nationalist community. She questioned if that support would be there for a return to bloodshed. The IRA, she speculated, might have dug its own grave as a paramilitary organization.

Patricia's faith in the IRA's responsiveness to the wishes of the community still strikes me as unduly optimistic. But her point remains valid. Even taking into account unresolved antagonisms and contrary goals, the vast majority of Belfast citizens, Protestant and Catholic alike, are far more sophisticated than the paramilitaries who profess to be defending, or advancing, their interests. Most people in Northern Ireland are, I suspect, reasonably tolerant and accepting of the need to negotiate compromise, rather than kill for status quo. In a sense, the city has evolved while the terrorists, acting pretty much as paramilitaries/freedom fighters have always acted in Ireland, remain frozen in the past. Of great importance has been the dogged emergence, apparent during the fifteen years I have been visiting Northern Ireland, of a secular, materialist, almost flashy Belfast. After decades of rectitude, the desire among people to dress sharply, eat better, have some fun outside of their houses and neighbourhoods, is healthy. Such irreverence — often confused with a lack of seriousness — may prove the strongest antidote to the fratricide that has kept the city, and the state built around it, in perpetual disarray.

ACKNOWLEDGEMENTS

I am eternally grateful to the McNallys for their generosity and co-operation. *The Last House of Ulster* makes no pretence towards objectivity; it is written out of love and respect for the family. If this book has a theme, it is values, and aside from my parents no individuals have had a greater impact on my own than the McNallys of North Belfast.

Thanks are also due to many individuals who helped with research. These include Sean McNally, Fred Heatley, Barra O Seaghdha, Denis Sampson and Eibhear Walshe. For general support, I am indebted to John Fraser and Iris Tupholme. A grant from the Canada Council made my trips to and from Belfast easier, as did the caretaking aid of Muriel and David Foran. Mary Ladky was, as ever, essential.

Dozens of books about Belfast and Northern Ireland were consulted during the writing process. The city has an exceptional literary culture, and continues to produce remarkable poets, novelists and chroniclers. Among the most helpful sources were Robert Johnstone's *Belfast*, C.E.B. Brett's *Housing a Divided Community* and *Buildings of Belfast*, Geoffrey Beattie's *We Are the People*, Christopher McGimpsey's *Bombs on Belfast*, and the fine Blackstaff Press anthology *The Rattle of the North*. The poetry of Ciaran Carson is invaluable to understanding the city. The monthly magazine *Fortnight* is obligatory reading as was, for me, their chronology of the Troubles, *Troubled Times*. For more general coverage I relied on J. Bowyer Bell's *The Irish Troubles* and several books by Conor Cruise O'Brien.

GLOSSARY

Anglo-Irish Agreement: 1985 agreement between London and Dublin that granted the republic a modest consultative role in Northern Irish affairs. Ineffectual at ground level.

"B" Specials: notorious Protestant auxiliary police force. Disbanded by the British government in 1971.

Broo: colloquial name for social security.

Camogie: version of hurling played by women.

Collins, Michael: charismatic leader during War of Independence, also known as Anglo-Irish war or, in Northern Ireland, the Tan war (1919–21). Led delegation to London to negotiate Anglo-Irish Treaty. Killed during the Civil War (1922–23).

"Crack": from the Irish. Infers high spirits, good fun, pleasant atmosphere.

Devlin, Bernadette: prominent civil-rights activist and republican. Elected to British parliament in 1969, at age twenty-two. Now known as Bernadette McAliskey.

Diplock courts: non-jury courts for paramilitary offences. Often relied on uncorroborated evidence supplied by "reformed" terrorists (supergrasses) in exchange for reduced sentences and/or relocation.

Downing Street Accord: joint declaration between London and Dublin in December 1993. Reaffirmed "constitutional guarantee" of Britain to Northern Ireland. Emphasized consent of Northern majority in any decision. Declared Britain's role to be a facilitator.

Emmett, Robert: leader of brief 1803 uprising. Executed in Dublin.

Fenians: nineteenth-century insurgent movement, both in Ireland and North America. Also used as derogatory term for Catholics.

IRB: Irish Republican Brotherhood. Secret nationalist group during nineteenth-century and first decades of twentieth-century. Influenced Irish Volunteers, who led Easter 1916 uprising. Placed members alongside newly formed guerilla IRA in 1919–21 conflict.

King Billy: William of Orange. Dutch prince who became joint English monarch with wife Mary in Glorious Revolution of 1688. Landed outside Belfast in June 1690 to lead army against deposed Stuart King James. Victory at Battle of Boyne completed conquest of Ireland.

Lough: Irish and Scottish term for lake, or bay of a sea.

MacSwiney, Terrence and Ashe, Thomas: republicans who died on hunger strikes during War of Independence. Became symbols of resistence to English rule. MacSwiney was Lord Mayor of Cork.

Molyneaux, James: head of reasonably moderate UUP (Ulster Unionist Party) since 1979.

Official IRA: original Irish Republican Army. At outbreak of Troubles, favoured political rather than military campaign. Largely absorbed into Marxist Workers Party after 1970 split that created Provisionals.

On the Blanket: campaign by republican prisoners during late 1970s to protest loss of prisoner-of-war status. Refers to refusal of prisoners to wear uniforms.

Paisley, Rev. Ian: founder-leader of the extremist DUP (Democratic Unionist Party) and fundamentalist Free Presbyterian Church. Has had enormous impact on affairs in Northern Ireland since mid-1960s, almost entirely negative.

The Pale: Fluctuating fourteenth-century line around Dublin that represented territory controlled by Anglo-Normans. Rest of country was Gaelic.

Pearse, Patrick and Connolly, James: leaders of 1916 Easter Uprising in Dublin. Pearse was a schoolteacher and poet, Connolly a labour leader. Their executions, along with those of fourteen other men, contributed to a shift in attitude towards armed rebellion against British rule.

Penal Laws: punitive laws that, after an initial period of "religious" enthusiasm following conquest of 1690, were directed at keeping property and political power out of Catholic hands.

Provisional IRA: the "IRA" to most North Americans. Also called "Provos" or "Provies" or "the Rah". In addition to conventional terrorism, also involved in recent years in racketeering, extortion and intimidation, largely directed towards its "own" community, often in loose business partnership with loyalist paramilitaries. Sinn Fein ("Ourselves Alone") serves as political wing.

Red Hand: in Ulster legend, two kings competed to be first to reach the shore of Ulster. One king ensured his victory by severing his limb and tossing it ahead. Loyalist symbol of resistance, determination.

RUC: The Royal Ulster Constabulary. Local police force for Northern Ireland. Ninety per cent Protestant.

SDLP: Social Democratic Labour Party. Co-founded in 1970 and still headed by moderate John Hume. Regularly wins a majority of Northern nationalist votes.

Shebeen: illegal drinking house.

"Shoot to Kill": unofficial policy of certain members of security forces. Republican suspects were executed, instead of arrested. Most lethal during 1980s.

Taigs: derogatory term for Catholics.

UDA: Ulster Defence Association. Largest loyalist paramilitary organization. Only recently made illegal.

UFF: Ulster Freedom Fighters. Cover for UDA members engaging in terrorist activities.

Ulster: misnomer. Technically, the province ceased to exist with Partition. Protestants retain the name, as do historians referring to the former nine-county territory, one of the rhetorical four green fields. (Other provinces are Munster, Leinster and Connaught.) There is no neutral name for Northern Ireland.

UVF: Ulster Volunteer Force. Loyalist paramilitary organization.

Young Ireland Movement: 1848 nationalist movement led by Thomas Davis. Culminated in brief, futile uprising.

BOOKS

Also from Saturday Night Books

Father Must by Rick Rofihe

Fever by Sharon Butala

Fresh Girls & Other Stories by Evelyn Lau

Getting Used to Dying by Zhang Xianliang

Green Grass, Running Water by Thomas King

Looking Around: A Journey Through Architecture
by Witold Rybczynski

*The Man-Eater of Punanai: A Journey of Discovery to the
Jungles of Old Ceylon* by Christopher Ondaatje

Marine Life by Linda Svendsen

Minus Time by Catherine Bush

The Saturday Night Traveller edited by George Galt

Sketches in Winter: A Beijing Postscript by Charles Foran

Stalin's Nose: Travels Around the Bloc by Rory MacLean

Voyages: At Sea With Strangers by Joan Skogan

The Way We Are by Margaret Visser

HarperCollins*PublishersLtd*